# Redeeming Gethsemane

*When Our Age of Loneliness
Meets a Woke Church*

## By Daniel K. Held

Copyright ©2021 by Daniel K. Held (Higher Ground Books & Media) All rights reserved. No part of this publication may be reproduced in any form, stored in a retrieval system, or transmitted in any form, or by any means (electronic, mechanical, photocopying, recording or otherwise) without prior permission by the copyright owner and the publisher of this book.

Scripture taken from the HOLY BIBLE, New Revised Standard Version.

Higher Ground Books & Media Springfield, Ohio.
http://highergroundbooksandmedia.com

Printed in the United States of America 2021

# Redeeming Gethsemane

*When Our Age of Loneliness
Meets a Woke Church*

# By Daniel K. Held

"Loneliness is proof that your innate search for connection is intact."

– **Martha Beck**

PREFACE

This book is written with one purpose in mind. To bring those of us who would follow Jesus into connection first with each other and then with those outside our immediate circle of friends and acquaintances. It is about Christian discipleship and about the mission of making new disciples in today's world.

To achieve this purpose, we must acknowledge that while life is taught in linear ways that produce nicely straight lines, it is learned in non-linear ways that involve steps forward and backward and then forward again. Books are written in a straightforward manner, but life is not lived in that same way. Life is more often lived in back-and-forth patterns far more circular than straight.

This may be especially true of Christian life and of the learning we call discipleship.

With this in mind, my suggestion is that the reader may best grasp the actual lessons of this book by reading in a uniquely circular pattern unfamiliar to most of us. The Introduction speaks for itself, but then the next 10 chapters and Conclusion may best be read in a back-and-forth movement to accommodate a unique 6-week small group discussion. Questions are provided in back designed to follow a uniquely non-linear approach to reading and learning.

Week One……. Chapters 1 and 6.

Week Two ……Chapters 2 and 7

Week Three… Chapters 3 and 8

Week Four ……Chapters 4 and 9

Week Five……. Chapters 5 and 10

Week Six ……. Introduction and Conclusion

ACKNOWLEDGEMENTS:

I would like to acknowledge each person who reached out to me with a willingness to share a story of personal loneliness. The courage you have shown to be vulnerable in this way inspires me beyond words. For your trust in me to place your stories within the sacred context each one deserves, I thank you. Your insights are beyond reproach as you have faced both bitter and better memories of Christ's church in today's age of loneliness. You motivate us all to stay awake, watch out, and pray with others who now walk where you once journeyed as well.

I would also like to thank those, too many to name, who expressed support for this writing project and its aim of stimulating our growth as disciples of Jesus. Your encouragement gave me a much-needed nudge to keep working when I, too, found my spirit willing but my flesh weak.

I would especially like to thank Rebecca Benston, whose tireless work and endless love in telling our stories brings redemption to more and more readers every year through "Higher Ground Books & Media." She is the most caring and devoted traditional publisher any writer could ever hope to meet. I feel blessed every day for having found her as my own woke church at a time when I was most tempted to abandon all hope as an author, despite God's call in my life.

## TESTIMONIALS

"Redeeming Gethsemane relates real life experiences to scripture to overcome loneliness and challenges us to wake up and live out the Gospel. Dan Held skillfully weaves these experiences to make the scripture come alive in new ways. A great study book!"

-- Donald L. Hayashi, past Associate General Secretary, General Council on Ministries of the United Methodist Church

"Dan Held offers an antidote to loneliness: hope. Using Gethsemane, the stories of Scripture, and the words of Jesus, Held paints a portrait of renewal desperately needed today. As a bonus, discussion questions make the book ideal for group study. Gethsemane gives hope!"

-- Thomas Jay Oord, author of *The Uncontrolling Love of God* and numerous other books

# INTRODUCTION

Aloneness and loneliness.

The differences are profound. As profound as those between privacy and abandonment, or between quietude and isolation. They are human experiences calling forth human need. How others respond to that need matters. Which is why this book is being written.

We live in an age of loneliness that too often is met with a response appropriate more for aloneness. By this I mean, our loneliness is too often met with disengagement and distance. That is the very thing we need during our times of aloneness, but quite different, even opposite, the need we bring to the experience of loneliness.

Response matters.

It has always mattered.

And to be entirely fair, ours is not the first age where a response to another's time of loneliness was largely met with disengagement and distance, instead of a much-needed connection and closeness. As far back as the first century in our Common Era, we have examples of lonely individuals finding themselves abandoned at the worst possible time. Isolated and offered "privacy" when the real need was for companionship and support.

Take the case of Jesus of Nazareth.

The Message Bible uses these words to describe his times of wanting to be left alone: "*As often as possible Jesus withdrew to out-of-the-way places for prayer.*" Several examples are found within the Christian New Testament Bible of such times and places. *"In the morning, while it was still very dark, he got up and went out to a deserted place, and there he prayed"* -- Mark 1:35. *"And after he had dismissed the crowds, he went up on the mountain by himself to pray. When evening came, he was there alone"* -- Matthew 14:23.

Being alone. Not so bad for Jesus, right? In fact, we get the impression he sometimes preferred it that way. He liked his privacy especially at times when he wanted to pray. He even taught his disciples the benefits of praying alone, as in Matthew 6:5-6, *"And whenever you pray, do not be like the hypocrites; for they love to stand and pray in the synagogues and at the street corners, so that they may be seen by others. Truly I tell you, they have received their reward. But whenever you pray, go into your room and shut the door and pray to your Father who is in secret; and your Father who sees in secret will reward you."*

So, what was up with Jesus when we read later on in Matthew 26, as well as in Mark 14 and Luke 22, that Jesus, by each synoptic account, took Peter, James, and John along with him to pray in the garden called *"Gethsemane"* on the night before he was to die? There he apparently invited them to pray with him. By all accounts, these charter members of his original Church of Jesus Christ of Nazareth went along with him. To a point.

The full response of this original small group of Church members involved what? They all fell asleep. Leaving Jesus alone to pray by himself.

Right response or not? What do you think?

Jesus often preferred to be left alone when he prayed. Rarely if ever did he ask others to come with him to pray. But this time he did.

Why?

Perhaps it was that Jesus preferred to be alone when he prayed out of love. But this time was different. He was praying out of fear. Fear made him feel loneliness, not aloneness. There's a difference.

Aloneness plus fear equals loneliness. And the loneliness of fear leads to temptation. Temptation to take control. Use fight or flight.

So, we're talking here about first of all a different response by Jesus himself. Normally, he preferred to pray alone. No fear. No loneliness. No sweating blood, as it were. No control issues, or any fight or flight response.

Yet, we're also talking here about a social response by what was, for all intents and purposes, the original Church of Jesus Christ of Nazareth. And here the response was unchanged. The Church was asleep at the proverbial switch, sleeping as if this was a time for Jesus to "just be alone" and praying the same as usual. Only Jesus was going through the unusual. He was responding differently. They were still responding the same.

Maybe you and I have been there where Jesus was. Abandoned by others at the very time we craved connection. Misunderstood in terms of wanting to be with others and not "just left alone" to get over it by ourselves. Maybe we've entered our own age of loneliness. Maybe we've felt as if we, too, were sweating blood while others were off taking it easy.

Maybe we've had our own Gethsemane moments.

And, then again, maybe we've been where Peter, James and John were. Tired. Sleepy. Oblivious to the cries of another person who we've interpreted as being "alone" instead of "lonely." Maybe you and I have also been the Church asleep at the switch during someone else's worst ever time of fear, loneliness, temptation.

If so, there is hope.

There is redemption available for our Gethsemanes in this world. Redemption for us when we are living in our own age of loneliness. And redemption for us when we are called to wake up and change our own response to others during their times of fear, loneliness, and temptation.

According to the Biblical story of Jesus in his own Gethsemane, he ran out of time after asking not once, not twice, but on the third try to wake the disciples who were asked to watch out and pray with him. By then it was too late.

The good news is that it's not too late for us. We can still redeem Gethsemane. We can still wake up and watch out. And pray.

You are about to read a book that is laid out in two parts. The first involves true life stories of others who, beside Jesus, were faced with feelings of abandonment while the Church, in effect, snoozed away opportunity and even necessity. You may relate. You may even say to yourself, "see, this is why I've had it with Church." Simply put, there are far too many people who, like Jesus, have found the very people counted on for support, the ones expected to just be there and to "watch out" and to pray with................ assuming he-she-we only wanted to be left alone again. Far too many people who, like Jesus, have felt misunderstood or even abandoned in this life's most critical moments. Let's call this reality **"Sins of Omission."**

Ah, but there is a part two to this book.

Read on and understand this: there are just as many true-life stories of others for whom the Church was there, was awake, was watching out, and was praying through it all. These proclaim something of great import in today's world, today's age of loneliness. That something is this: when the church connects with the least of these Jesus has called his own brothers and sisters, it re-connects with Jesus himself. It reconciles and restores. Atones. It heals that painful emotion. It even forgives and lives to love again. And it lets go of fear.

Let's call this reality **"Signs of Redemption."**

From sins to signs. They are all "real" in our lives. They transform us from our fear stories to our love stories. They are the stories you are about to read.

PART ONE            **"Sins of Omission"**

*Then they also will answer, 'Lord, when was it that we saw you hungry or thirsty or a stranger or naked or sick or in prison, and did not take care of you?' Then he will answer them, 'Truly I tell you, just as you did not do it to one of the least of these, you did not do it to me.'*

**(MT 25:44-45)**

Chapter 1

Here is something you have never asked your search engine to locate: celebrities who prefer to be alone. Try it sometime. I did just out of curiosity and learned something new.

A website about celebrities in the area of theater and cinematic arts appeared near the top of the page. Entertainers. People who reach out through their own unique artistry and touch the public at some emotional level provide a very unique service of empathy. Their audience of spectators is able to see themselves in their on-stage or on-screen persona only. There they create a kind of pseudo-bond with the public. Perhaps too close of a bond. And so, quite often, according to the website https://www.theadventurouswriter.com, these very celebrities identify themselves as introverts who prefer, if at all possible, to be left alone.

As I mentioned in Introduction, Jesus quite often preferred to be left alone. Not saying he was an introvert, nor one who stood silent, but he seemed to crave his own privacy after being around people all day.

Jesus was also a celebrity.

No, he wasn't into the theatrical arts but was really far more eclectic. He performed in fields ranging from the culinary to the healing arts, was an expert storyteller and a gifted motivational speaker. His road tour had a collection of what today we call "roadies" or what the Bible called "disciples." But what made Jesus the total celebrity that he was in the Bible were the audiences he would draw when on tour. Today we'd call them "groupies," perhaps, but to Jesus they were, to borrow his own contemporary metaphor, "sheep" in search of a shepherd. At any rate, his fans followed him around from one venue to another. Like sheep following a reliable shepherd.

The Gospel of Mark tells about Jesus's first ever road tour. We read about the crowds Jesus was already drawing in the town of Capernaum several miles up from the north shore of the Sea of Galilee. Worn out by all those crowds, he went off into a solitary place to pray one morning. It was early. He got away with it for a while, but like perhaps most celebrities he was eventually spotted. His cover blown by his own disciples, they offered up words for him that every introverted celebrity in the world may have heard, **"everyone is looking for you!"** (Mark 1:37)

Jump to the next scene. Jesus gets his disciples, his "roadies," together and launches his first road tour. Timing is everything. They're doing the towns and villages around the larger region of Galilee. He had this gig in one of the village synagogues, where Jesus spotted his first ever lost sheep in the crowd. Jesus is noted in the overall biblical story as having a special attraction to such lost sheep because he saw them as having a loneliness problem. It was as if he had a special nose for loneliness or went looking for it among the crowds in his audience. But just as special was the way in which lonely people in his day sensed they, each one, actually mattered to Jesus. If nobody else would have much to do with them, they would seek out Jesus. Like a lost sheep seeks out a shepherd.

So, we're reading along in Mark's first chapter when we come across this amazing story: ***A leper came to him begging him, and kneeling he said to him, "If you choose, you can make me clean." Moved with pity, Jesus stretched out his hand and touched him, and said to him, "I do choose. Be made clean!" Immediately the leprosy left him, and he was made clean.***

Who do you suppose were the loneliest people in any crowd when Jesus, the celebrity, was on tour? Who in the synagogue is most apt to be sitting alone? Or standing off to the side? Who comes closest to feeling neglected or abandoned by the "in" people who "belong" in the building?

Probably the lepers. Or in this case, leper. Alone.

Having caught an incurably contagious skin disease of pandemic proportions, this leper may have felt cursed like nobody else in the audience at that particular synagogue where Jesus had just spoken and performed his powerful healing arts. Jesus was known to have targeted those in his audience who were tormented mentally. Interesting that Mark, author of the earliest New Testament Gospel, situated these folks in attendance at the synagogues. As if to say, you're here among the religious people but you are lonely and secretly tormented in your own minds, and I know who you are because you matter to me. I, Jesus, have come here to help you.

If Jesus could help those tormented with mental problems, surely, he would understand the mental torment that went along with the skin disease of leprosy. Yet this particular leper was relegated to the back of that line. The last of the least, as it were.

Somebody always has to go last.

Going last means risking that the healer could say "my time's up" and leave before you even got to the plate. The last of the least are used to being turned away. The expert says, "I'll take one more question" and yours is the 3rd hand to go up in the crowd. If you're a leper, you might as well leave now. Alone. Try not to touch anybody on the way out.

After all of the mentally ill are treated, Jesus will be out of time. Just give it up.

Only Jesus wasn't. And the leper didn't.

And finally, it was his turn. The lonely leper could now approach Jesus with his request. He would approach Jesus filled with the kind of awe and humility only a true celebrity might require. Begging. Kneeling. Saying to Jesus, *"If you choose, you can make me clean."*

Jesus did something unusual, even beyond remarkable, considering the nature of this poor man's loneliness problem. He reached out and touched him. And in so doing the leprosy itself did what other people had been doing all along. Mark writes," the *leprosy left him alone."* Used to being left lonely by people who refused to even come near, his disease had now left him alone.

Finally, aloneness without the loneliness. Big difference.

Back in the year 1963 a Christian musical celebrity, Bill Gaither, wrote these words made popular among many joining in song:

*Shackled by a heavy burden*
*'Neath a load of guilt and shame*
*Then the hand of Jesus touched me*
*And now I am no longer the same*

*He touched me, oh, he touched me*
*And oh the joy that floods my soul!*
*Something happened, and now I know*
*He touched me, and made me whole*

That was Jesus doing what Jesus did. Searching out the lost sheep from among the hostile or indifferent crowds. Touching those no one else would ever think of touching. Casting out the problem in order to bring in the person. An art in itself. The healing artistry, indeed, the celebrity, of Jesus at its best.

Now it's time for a bigger question. Are we as Christians doing what Jesus did?

Are we staying until the last of the least is served? Are we waiting for those who are "*shackled by a heavy burden?*" Are we making whole those who are broken?

Am I doing what Jesus did? I've had to ask that of myself.

One way I could improve my own life and testimony in this area was to write this book. It would force me to get out away from the crowd, the 90 and 9 referred to elsewhere by Jesus in his storytelling and find a lost sheep. Someone flying under the social radar. Someone standing at the back of the line. The third hand going up when there was only time for one more question. Would I be willing to search out the ones who remain untouched? Ignored? Disconnected?

I can assure any reader who might be interested, if one goes looking for a lost sheep today there will be dozens of them to choose from. No, hundreds. No, millions. For we live today in an age of loneliness.

One person I found in my own search is a man named Erik. In writing to me, Erik describes himself in these words:

*"I was brought up in a traditional [Protestant] home with my father being a minister. Church every Sunday was expected. I went to a* [denominationally affiliated] *college and* [then post-graduate] *seminary. I pursued a career as a chaplain and served as a hospital and hospice chaplain for almost 30 years. I found the work incredibly meaningful and enjoyed having colleagues to relate to. Church was still an important part of my connection to faith.*

*Later in my career I was laid off from my job and despite many attempts to get back into it, I never came to any fruition. Around that time, I was also going through a divorce……. There was a time of six months where I was homeless even though I was working. I was sending all my money to my ex so she would have a home to keep the kids in. I never shared with them that I was sleeping in my office. I never shared this with anyone at work either. I found some really creative and crafty ways to survive.*

*I rarely go to church anymore. When I was struggling with the job loss, I found the needed support from church lacking. They had a great theology, but it just stayed a theology. Going to church meant less and less. Occasionally I would be touched by a musical piece, but that was about it. When I moved to another state and got another job, I tried some churches, but I had the same experience and found myself bored and disconnected."*

In speaking directly with Erik about this experience, I asked why he kept going back to churches hoping for connection. I wondered, too, why he felt bored and disconnected in that process. He shared with me how, in his worst times of loneliness, he was driven all the more to seek some kind of reliable connection. By this time, his parents were aging and unable, for reasons of their own, to offer assistance or to display any kind of real compassion for him. Homeless and estranged, he had his own reasons for feeling a bit like the leper who went to see Jesus. Hoping to connect. Hoping for understanding and the touch of a friendly hand. Someone who would even ask about him; maybe watch out and pray with him; maybe question whether he was okay or not; perhaps someone willing to find out that he was not. Something beyond the good music, the good preaching, the **"good theology."**

A personal touch. Erik kept looking for what he needed the most. Someone to care that he was without work. Or without housing. Family? Church? No one was awake to his life crisis. Finally, he just quit going to church altogether.

Erik goes on to tell of how he turned away from even trying to find another church he could connect with on a personal level. He took his search into nature. He writes, *"so on the weekends I found another church. I would go hiking or biking in nature. I hiked some segments of the Appalachian Trail and found that my mind was at a much better place doing this. Even the bike trails left me with a sense of wonder at nature and all of creation. I explored painting pictures and photography of my hikes. I became really interested in barns and was intrigued by their personalities. In short, my faith became more private but more meaningful.*

I think of how it must have been for the man with leprosy whom Jesus connected with. The three synoptic Gospels vary in detail somewhat, but they all noted that this was the first leper to ever approach Jesus. His faith in Jesus was what he, too, may have thought of as private but meaningful. Maybe he attended other synagogue services; maybe he didn't. But Jesus would be at this synagogue on this day. He would try to connect. And he would succeed.

For Erik, I find it interesting to note that his private faith was able to grow even apart from any church affiliation. And that he was able to then do something with his faith that brought him into connection quite apart from local churches.

He writes, *"I* [started] *a group on Facebook that became my 'congregation.' It was made up of all kinds of people from regular church attenders to atheists, to people in various forms of recovery to people just searching. So, I have a different 'church' for myself and a different 'tribe' to associate with. I do not reject any of what I learned or experienced in my traditional life or faith, but I have grown to where I need to be in this moment for others and myself."*

At last count, the Facebook group Erik started and uses to connect with the all-too-often disillusioned in today's world had reached 894 members and counting. More than he had ministered to in any of his 30 years of service as a Chaplain.

There are indeed places other than formalized faith communities or churches to find cures for loneliness these days. These may include hiking or biking trails, or any number of other opportunities to feel connected to that which is larger than ourselves. Even social media groups.

But here's the point.

When loneliness meets connection, being alone becomes far less preferred. Instead, reaching out and offering new connection with others is the more likely outcome. Which brings us back to the story of Jesus, the celebrity, on his first road tour as noted by Mark's Gospel. It seems Jesus advised the man who had come to him with leprosy to *"see that you say nothing to anyone; but go, show yourself to the priest, and offer for your cleansing what Moses commanded, as a testimony to them."*

In the Gospels of both Mark and Luke, we get a sense this did not happen. No return to the synagogue to see any Priest at all. Instead, the now ex-leper did something more akin to what Erik more recently did. He went about broadcasting far and wide that even loneliness can be healed, and people can be connected, and touched, in new and exciting ways. For Erik it was starting a new Facebook group for others like himself. For the leper in the story with Jesus, we read, *"…… he went out and began to proclaim it freely, and to spread the word, so that Jesus could no longer go into a town openly but stayed out in the country; and people came to him from every quarter."*

So much for Jesus ever finding it easy being alone from that day on. Once people found him easy to meet and connect with, staying for those at the end of the line, touching even the untouchables, people would approach from all directions.   Hanging on like groupies.   And giving Jesus a need for privacy like only today's best-known celebrities may understand.

Chapter 2

The experience of loneliness Jesus suffered in the garden of Gethsemane prior to his arrest was a painful disconnect with his closest disciples. But that was not his first disconnect with those he had previously trusted. Not even the first one that week.

The three synoptic Gospels describe an earlier event that week in which Jesus entered the most public place among the Temple courtyards in Jerusalem and essentially declared war against the Chief Priests. It was there, in this Holy place, that Jesus witnessed a price gouging routine conducted by Temple officials. Once a year, on Passover holiday, every Jew had to come from near and far to pay a Temple tax. In shekels. Yet, Jews arriving in Jerusalem from outside the region had only their own currency to use. So, step one meant getting in line for currency exchange. This cost the "foreign" Jews dearly. The exchange rate was exorbitant. But once at the Temple to pay that tax, one also needed to pay two separate animal offerings to God. One was a burnt offering of personal submission to the Holy One, and the other was a sin offering to attain forgiveness for one's transgressions of the Law within the prior year.

Oh, and the animals presented for sacrifice had to be approved by the Temple inspectors as "unblemished."

What raised the ire of Jesus was this: the majority of Jews from outside Jerusalem were poor enough that they could not bring, say, an unblemished male lamb for offering. Provisions in the Law were such that they would have to buy a pair of cheap pigeons or turtledoves and present them instead. They could be had for a rather low price outside the city walls.

Fair enough.

But the family of Annas the High Priest had rigged the game. The Temple inspectors were charged with finding a blemish on each bird brought in from outside. But no worries. Unblemished doves were for sale inside by the Temple Priests. For twice the price paid outside the gates. It was price gouging. Everyone knew it. But Jesus did something about it.

Jesus, we're told in the Gospels, *"overturned the tables of the money changers and the seats of those who sold doves"* (Mark 11:15) while reminding both buyers and sellers alike that, per Isaiah 56:7, *"these I will bring to my holy mountain, and make them joyful in my house of prayer; their burnt offerings and their sacrifices will be accepted on my altar; for my house shall be called a house of prayer for all peoples."*

Jesus was just now starting into his rant. To be continued.

There was also the point made by the prophet Jeremiah, *"has this house, which is called by my name, become a den of robbers in your sight? You know, I too am watching, says the Lord"* (Jer. 7:11).

Rant finally over.

Only the fourth Gospelist, John, added that Jesus actually drove these Temple officials out of their court using his own homemade whip (John 2:15). I guess you could call that a disconnect. Jesus and his own people, the leaders within his own Jewish religion. A prelude to loneliness.

"Have you ever noticed that people who are disturbed by social injustice enough to fight for it, not just speak about it, are on a pathway to loneliness? That was Jesus, for sure, days before he ever set foot in the garden of Gethsemane for prayer with his worn-out disciples.

William Barclay, the late, renowned Biblical Professor from the U. of Glasgow, notes that where the injustice of price gouging for poor Jews coming as foreign pilgrims for tax and religious sacrifice was concerned, Jesus wasn't the first to notice it all. Writings in the Talmud preceding Jesus included those of Rabbi Simon ben Gamaliel insisting that the Temple price for a pair of doves be cut in half. But to no avail.

It isn't as though injustice goes unnoticed or even unopposed in our world. But there's a peculiar difference between those who write about it and maybe speak out against it, and those who make their own whips. Do you know what I mean?

Those who are so disturbed by injustice that they go about making actual changes, turning the tables, as it were? They are destined, later if not sooner, for loneliness even among those who are otherwise mildly perturbed by that same injustice. Which describes my friend, Linda.

I met Linda while serving in retirement as an associate on staff tasked with Congregational Care. She was active in various areas of lay leadership, including helping to care for the infirmed in their homes and hospitals throughout our local parish. I saw her do some rather amazing things in attending to the needs of our members. On one occasion, Linda called me from the Hospice bedside of a lady named Jan. Linda had such a heart for the hurting that she did all in her power to help them, all the way to the end sometimes. No longer able to bring Jan's favorite foods over to her home in hopes of coaxing a few bites from which to draw strength, Linda was relegated to now doing a bedside vigil gently wiping Jan's brow with a warm, damp cloth. And now, as Jan's death neared, Linda phoned me to say, "I think it's time. Jan needs a pastor to be here with her. Can you come?" My reply is one I had forgotten, but Linda has not. She says I assured her that Jan already had a pastor with her.

In any event, Linda went about praying for some further guidance from above in the matter of her role in church leadership. With encouragement from our Senior Pastor, she decided to enter the pathway to become a local licensed Pastor within our church denomination. She diligently went about various required studies and took on a remarkable passion for helping right the wrongs of other people in the community. She had a heart bigger than what one typically finds even within the best of local churches. She worked hard. She served passionately. And she fought for justice everywhere near and far. Harder than most anyone else was willing to fight.

Then Linda hit what I can only describe as a wall.

It was the kind of wall that disconnects the determined from those who are merely interested. That separates those who are mildly perturbed from those who are passionately disturbed by a particular injustice. And I'm not so sure this doesn't happen more often than we know within the church. Fighters for justice may experience a loneliness few go on to ever express.

Linda, however, is given to expression and was, upon request, willing to place in writing what her loneliness apart from her own church actually felt like. Her story goes like this:

*I became a late-in-life second-career pastor some years ago. It was in both exhilaration and terror that I took this on. I'd felt called all my life, but always found ways to avoid that holy responsibility. Who was I to represent God? More broken than most, I came to the ministry with a decidedly checkered past. More than checkered: plaid, with crisscrosses of sins, failures, debaucheries, ruined opportunities, weaknesses, betrayals—basically, just a big hot mess. It took me a good year to hear "Pastor Linda" without cringing inwardly at the knowledge of how unworthy I was of that appellation.*

*Finally, though, I learned to hear it just as a job description. A job title. A pastor oversees a Christian church. We prepare and deliver the worship message. We tend to our people. We visit homes and hospitals, take care of baptisms and deaths, perform weddings, attend meetings and conferences, and do our best to herd a disparate lot of humans along a clear path to becoming our highest beings. An honorable profession, a high calling, but in the end, "pastor" is like cook, mail carrier, CEO, parent, janitor—it's what we do, not who we are.*

*Still, despite the joy, the enthusiasm, the eagerness with which I threw myself into this new role, it became the loneliest, most disillusioning years of my life. We should never see how the sausage is made if we want to go on enjoying the taste.*

*I can describe the primary source of this malaise through the relationship I had with my senior pastor, and I will, as a symbolic truth. But in fact, no individual deserves the full blame.*

*I've been out of the ministry now for almost four years, but I am not healed. Not by a long shot. And when I meditate on this, when I examine myself and others, when I look over the whole time, my eye still drifts over to that man, although I know he is merely the symbol of a greater ill.*

*I liked this pastor. Respected him. He was my mentor and teacher. I learned a great deal from him. I valued his friendship. And in the years, I served under him in his church, his support was steadfast, warm, encouraging. I relied on it.*

*What changed? I still don't know and may never know. Somehow, when I became pastor of my own congregation, he began to see me as a competitor. Difficult. He began to say very hurtful things to me, exclude me from meetings, gatherings, opportunities to speak. At one point, in the presence of colleagues, he said "no wonder your daughter wants nothing to do with you," referencing a decade-long estrangement from my daughter, a thing he knew only from private pastoral counseling with me. He told me I was only a quarter time hire and not worth the trouble, though I gave my church 90 hours a week.*

*He became increasingly hostile, threatening, sneering, mocking, dismissive. In meetings with other pastors and administrators, he was openly in opposition to me, not even trying to hide his impatience with my presence. I'd finish a report or comment and he'd say, "are you done?" then proceed to ignore me throughout the rest of the meeting. Many times.*

*It got bad enough that he finally convened a meeting of my parishioners to get me fired. At that time, they declined which did not, I assure you, extinguish the fire of his determination. I began the formal process of filing claim for a hostile work environment as well at working through my district support, such as it was, to foster a reconciliation.*

*And it's not that my district did nothing. Within their framework of operation, I do believe attempts were made on my behalf. The district superintendent at the time seemed to take my issues seriously. His successor offered to teach me the seminary classes this pastor was teaching so that my academic work could be treated fairly.*

*But this is the junction where this senior pastor is less at fault individually than the system as a whole. All organized religion, not just Christianity, is a hotbed of dirty politics, in-fighting, jockeying for place, defense of their own, and when threatened, they close ranks.*

*Churches, in the final analysis, are businesses, and are run like businesses: established hierarchy, entrenched methods and patriarchy, unspoken but understood and practiced rules of engagement that do not reflect the love of God, but the love of order, position, power and influence. In the business of church, it is not Who you know, but who you know.*

*There is no desire in me to present myself as an innocent victim of the Big Bad Wolf. I confess to being headstrong, opinionated, goal-focused, and no less prone to thinking I'm right than any other person. It would be a vast understatement to describe me as occasionally difficult. Stubborn. Intractable. Confronting. Mea culpa. Guilty as charged, and then some.*

*But my whole heart was in that job. That life. There was no moment throughout that walking through the purifying fire of ministry that was not a conscious, deliberate and daily—even hourly—decision and choice. I would burn, and gladly, for the joy of serving.*

*What I didn't know, couldn't know, still cannot come fully to grips with, was that I would not just burn. I would burn up. Burn out.*

*I lost that battle. I've made what peace with it I can, still a work in progress. But I am changed by it. In a lifetime of struggles and losses, nothing matched seeing my church turn its back on me, all my work crumble, my reputation left in tatters. There is a pall over me now that casts its shadow on even the sunniest days. A sorrow unmeasurable. And an essential, existential loneliness I fear will never leave me.*

My purpose in sharing Linda's account of her own loneliness is to suggest that Gethsemane for some, even within the church, comes about over the course of time when their own idealistic zeal hits a wall of separation or disconnect. Those willing to fight for justice with their own homemade whips are destined to feel abandoned by those less militant, less radical, less passionate. While wearing out others of lesser passion, they may find themselves burning out themselves within their own sense of pastoral call. They find the church too indifferent to their pressured demand for social justice, too complacent to the pains of other persons, and asleep in the face of an alarming crisis in their own backyard. They may feel Linda's same loneliness.

Chapter 3

The 15th chapter of Matthew has always been a bit of a challenge to wrestle within my own mind. It reads like a dramatic play in three Acts. Act I, scene I, involves a group of Pharisees and religious leaders from the "legal department" in the home office up in Jerusalem. They had arrived in Galilee, the place even they may have regarded as being "the sticks," for the purpose of, let's say, having a little talk with Jesus.

What about?

Well, rumor had it back at headquarters that this itinerant rabbi named Jesus was going around violating the Jewish laws of cleanliness. His disciples were going so far as to eat their food without having washed their hands.

This was a scene of confrontation. It involved the ultimate insiders, the honchos called Pharisees from the home office, and the outsiders. That would be Jesus, and his disciples.

The Bible is full of such drama straight out of central casting.

As in other such scenes in the New Testament, Jesus and his cohorts were always wearing the metaphorical uniform of the outsiders. If Jesus were a baseball manager and his disciples the team, they'd all be wearing the gray uniforms throughout. Even when they were the home team as in this first scene of Matthew 15, the Pharisees were the team in white. Jesus and his team wore the gray "traveling" uniforms. They could use the smaller clubhouse and the "other" dugout, if one might apply baseball metaphors in our thinking.

So here were the big guys, the insiders, the "always wearing the home uniforms" officials from Jerusalem paying Jesus a visit. Delivering the reprimand. Confronting him and his fellow outsiders about their sinful violation of the Hebrew Torah.

Except that, per usual, Jesus didn't receive his reprimand terribly well. He countered the Pharisees confrontation about handwashing with his own reprimand of his would-be bosses' sinful violation of the Hebrew Torah when it came to honoring their father and mother. Let's just say Jesus was, er, insubordinate. Bosses always hate that. All insiders hate that about all outsiders. Remember, Jesus and his followers were always cast in that lesser role in such dramas as Matthew 15. Cast as the "would be villains" getting their comeuppance from the assigned Pharisees. If only Jesus had been more, well, subordinate. More remorseful.

Then in that same chapter, scene two, the disciples tried talking Jesus down a notch or two, as if to shy away from the whole confrontation. Perhaps they were intimidated by the Pharisees when, verse 12, they said to Jesus, *"Do you know that the Pharisees took offense when they heard what you said?"*

It is at this point in Act I, scene two, where Jesus tells a parable of sorts. Ends like this. *"It is not what goes into the mouth that defiles a person, but it is what comes out of the mouth that defiles."* (15:11) Peter, who is arguably the top disciple or church team leader, didn't get it. *"But Peter said to Jesus, 'explain this parable to us.'"* (15:15) To which Jesus utters this line in response to Peter, *"Are you still without understanding?"* (15:16)

Act I then ends with Jesus voicing these final lines in the closing scene of verses 17-20: "**Do you not see that whatever goes into the mouth enters the stomach, and goes out into the sewer? But what comes out of the mouth proceeds from the heart, and this is what defiles. For out of the heart come evil intentions, murder, adultery, fornication, theft,**

**false witness, slander. These are what defile a person, but to eat with unwashed hands does not defile."**

Insubordination was never more straight-forward to the point.

Next in Act II, scene one opens with Jesus and his disciples having traveled out of Galilee and into the former Greek territory of Phoenicia, visiting the cities of Tyre and Sidon. Even there Jesus was recognized by a Greek (Syrophoenician, technically) mother who pleaded for his help on behalf of her daughter. This particular Mom was quite animated, apparently, because the scene continues with the disciples of Jesus (think "original church") advising Jesus to send the lady away "for she keeps shouting after us." (15:23) Here was a mother so determined to fight for her daughter's health and welfare that she next got on her knees, pleading, "Lord, help me." At this point, Jesus engages the lady in conversation as if to explain that he was on vacation and that his work in ministry was with the lost sheep of Israel back home.

How Jesus reportedly explained this has always bothered or at least puzzled me. I still feel that way.

Jesus *"answered, 'it is not fair to take the children's food and throw it to the dogs.'"* (15:26) I mean, could Jesus have picked a worse metaphor to use just then?

Yet at this point, the scene takes a dramatic turn. Because earlier in this 15th chapter the disciples, or at least Peter -- again, the team leader for what amounted to Christ's entire church -- didn't have faith enough to understand a simple parable. Now in this scene a far more complex parable and metaphor was spoken by Jesus and, without hesitation, this first Gentile person in recorded history to hear a saying of Jesus, expresses her complete understanding. *"She said, 'yes, Lord, yet even the dogs eat the crumbs that fall from their masters' table.'"* (15:27) To which Jesus replied, *"Woman, great is your faith! Let it be done for you as you wish."* (15:28)

Now remember what I noted earlier about insiders and outsiders? Here's where in Act II the plot twists back around. The evangelist Matthew writes of this turn-about in which Jesus was the insider from the Roman province of Galilee visiting this Greek province of Phoenicia. Larger context: the previous Greco-Roman Wars had found Rome victorious. Check the history books, if you don't believe me. Greeks were "losers" and anyone from a Roman province would be deemed "the home team," even when they were visiting inside Greek territory, as Jesus and his disciples were now doing upon their visits to Tyre and Sidon.

If you're looking for a more contemporary scene of comparison closer to home, try picturing a California tourist visiting Tijuana and encountering a beggar from Mexico. It's all about an imbalance of power. The tourist is the powerful insider, the beggar the poor outsider, even in his own homeland. But at first Christ's own church offers resistance. ***"Send her away, for she keeps shouting after me."***

Yep. That sounds like me on the one occasion my wife and I had to visit Tijuana. Felt like I was the insider with the home team uniform and the Mexican native was, well, the outsider in waiting.

Only Jesus handles the insider role differently. He, though at first hesitant, gives the outsider woman all that she asks for and then some. Pays her the supreme compliment of having "great faith!" For she was able to understand his most complex, troubling, puzzling parable even better than his own disciples, the church, did. In so doing, Jesus set a new standard for how insiders, like his church, are to deal with outsiders in need. Because these outsiders may understand more quickly and with even greater faith.

Which leads to the second or final scene in Act II. Jesus returns home and ascends to a mountain top from where he continues to heal everyone of every type of affliction.

Now comes Act III. And the final scene of this drama Matthew depicted in chapter 15. It's the scene where Jesus was still busy healing the multitudes, which reportedly amounted to about 4,000 people. Hungry people up there on the mountain. People in need of food. But with no place in which to first wash their hands. And a defiant Jesus who fed the people anyway. Why? Because *"it is not what goes into the mouth that defiles a person, but it is what comes out of the mouth that defiles."* (15:11)

Yet again, Jesus is joined with the outsiders against the insiders and enforcers from the home office. Had they been there, they would never have approved of his miraculous feeding of the 4,000 on that day in a place without suitable handwashing facilities. Turns out that sanitation, contrary to Act I, scene one, is not God's main concern for humanity. This is how Matthew 15 ends, but I wonder if such a drama doesn't play out on similar stages around the world in every generation. And not always with a woke church in such a redeeming role.

An associate of mine, Betty, is from a nearby town where she lived through a drama of her own as she recounts with me in writing. Hers also had scenes of having, as a mother, to fight for her daughter's health and welfare from the position of "outsider." In her powerful words, *"perhaps the loneliest time of my life was when I was going through my divorce and a very difficult custody hearing. I felt as though most of my church family stepped back and became unavailable."*

Remember the time in Matthew 15 when the disciples wanted more distance from that Greek Mom with the demonized daughter she was pleading for Jesus to help?

Betty's outsider status seemed clear to her. She writes, *"*n*ot that they had ever really felt like 'family,' but those with whom I'd been close didn't seem to step up and show support. In fact, one of the elders had even said to me that they would pray for a reconciliation in my marriage. I remember thinking that this was really not appropriate given that they* *didn't know the reasons why I was divorced, and they also hadn't suffered through the agony I faced while I was dealing with making that difficult decision. Marriage was not something I took lightly, and I certainly hadn't made the decision to leave the marriage without some intense prayer and many sleepless nights."*

With that, Betty's own drama continues with this scene from her own mind. *"At that time my greatest temptation was to leave the church. They were so entrenched in catch-phrase Christianity that they weren't reaching out in a way that was helpful or Godly. In fact, they were very judgmental. Many of the women in the church were younger and had been in church their entire lives. Their parents had been in church and so, they were brought up within the securely padded walls of the church and married off before they had the chance to engage in any sinful behaviors. They didn't understand what it was like to find Jesus without directions. There were no lions in their dens. There was no fire in their furnace. Instead of seeing themselves as the woman at the well, I truly believe they fancied themselves the living water itself. Very concerned with the production, but not the product. Sadly, there was an awful lot of Martha and very little Mary."*

And if I might add, while seeking my own understanding of that scene from Betty's own past, an awful lot of Gethsemane loneliness as she sat through the courtroom drama of a threatened loss of maternal custody because her daughter's father resented having to otherwise continue paying child support.

Betty's church had, like that original church belonging to Jesus himself, come along just so far with her before, in effect, choosing to sleep through the loneliness of her courtroom fears and temptations. She could have used a church beside her in prayer at that time.

By way of further sharing, Betty recalls that her church had been going through other difficulties of their own at this same time, as if to give their disciples some benefit of the doubt. Their building was changing ownership, and this had already pushed out the pastor and about half the congregation. Being totally frank about her situation, Betty was already at a point where she was ready to move on and find a different church.

But remember the Greek woman of *"great faith,"* as pronounced by Jesus in Matthew 15?

Times of Gethsemane loneliness are harder when one is the "outsider" others would prefer to distance from or ignore. Harder but no more impossible. Not when great faith is involved. And it was most definitely involved in Betty's personal story.

Like the outsider and presumably single Mom of Matthew 15, fighting for her own daughter's health and welfare by directing her faith toward Jesus, Betty also persisted. Never lost faith, even if at times it felt like she and her daughter were crumbs falling from the master's table. In her loneliness, Betty's faith stayed strong. Leave her church? Probably. Leave her faith in Jesus? Never.

Like Jesus, Betty was no stranger to praying alone, when necessary. Gethsemane for her, while lonely, was no deal breaker. It was far more difficult than it might have been had the church been there praying with her in her time of fearful temptation. Far more difficult!

But difficulty, even the most difficult age of loneliness, is never the end of our story. Note how Betty continues in sharing her own. *"I had spent nearly thirty years away from the church before finding this one; so leaving it was painful, but it had to be done. Since I had found my way back to God [through Jesus], I had been very intent on hearing His voice and doing what He was telling me to do. One of the most important things I had learned was that people will always disappoint us; God is the only one who will never let us down. It really didn't matter that the church had let me down. Nothing was going to stand in the way of my relationship with Christ at that point. I had spent too much time away from Him and I was never going to let other people pull me back into the pit."*

You're probably wondering by now. Did Betty lose custody of her daughter in court?

No.

Like the story of the Syrophoenician mother in Matthew 15, great faith paid off in the lives of Mom and daughter alike. It was a fight worth fighting. And winning.

Thank you, Jesus!

Even when the church is not there for us in our loneliness, God is there. Not to take our cup away from us but to empower us upward and onward to even better times than before. Regardless of what then happens to the church's own "insiders."

And now notice how Betty chooses to bring closure into her own story in the wake of Gethsemane loneliness: *"I still feel called to help people have more of an understanding of who God is and what He does rather than who the church is and what the church is trying to do; as these things don't always line up with one another. Although this type of evangelism is a bit lonely in terms of congregants, it is never lonely in terms of the presence of God. So, I'll gladly stay out here in the wilderness preparing for the work He wants me to do until He tells me to get in there and get it done. As for the church, they're still sleeping...and having nightmares, no doubt."*

Chapter 4

The writer of the Old Testament book of Ecclesiastes confronts an age-old problem involving the lonely worker. Upon looking at the vanities of life here on earth, that author was sure to include the person who suffers loneliness in the workplace. Be it a sole proprietor or a common employee showing up day in and day out for assignment, the workplace can have its own loneliness in any age. In many if not most cases, it is the last place the church follows even its own members.

Loneliness among the unemployed and under-employed is an all-too common malady. But the same amount of personal angst can accompany those whose work feels utterly vain or futile.

Notice how the matter is dealt with in these verses from Ecclesiastes 4:
*Again, I saw vanity under the sun: the case of solitary individuals, without sons or brothers; yet there is no end to all their toil, and their eyes are never satisfied with riches. "For whom am I toiling," they ask, "and depriving myself of pleasure?" This also is vanity and an unhappy business.*

The writer then goes on to explain.

*Two are better than one, because they have a good reward for their toil. For if they fall, one will lift up the other; but woe to one who is alone and falls and does not have another to help.*

I can recall from my prior work in pastoral ministry having an opportunity to visit a member of one congregation who was afflicted with autism. I will call him Dale. Then in his mid-forties, Dale was living within an adult group home but gainfully employed in a sheltered workshop environment where his ability to perform wrote manual tasks in the performance of piece-work manufacturing paid him pennies per accurate piece. One day I showed up to his workplace to visit him unannounced. His immediate supervisor led me to Dale's station and I was greeted, as customary, without any eye contact by Dale. However, his smiling face never beamed brighter! He was thrilled that I would come to visit and to learn of how he performed this important manufacturing task every day of the week. He proudly told his co-workers I was his Pastor Dan and for every Sunday that followed my visit I would get Dale's report of how many pieces he had produced in the previous pay period. The same report several times over! To Dale, work meant everything. Social connection, personal purpose, and a little extra spending money.

I seldom if ever visited the jobsite of the far more common parishioner. The ones who took little if any pride in their workplace activities. I rarely found anyone like Dale so eager to "talk shop" with me on Sunday mornings in the good-bye line at any sanctuary doors. Were I to ever broach the subject with other congregants of how things were going at work, I would often hear this two-word answer: "They're going." On fewer occasions, I would hear things like "really busy," or perhaps "really slow" or the occasional "they're going great!" Where I failed in retrospect as a pastor was to follow the too frequent "they're going" with a subsequent call to explore what things were "really" like these days at the office, the plant, etc. It was rare that I ever made workplace visits as a pastor. I'd go to the hospital but rarely the jobsite despite evidence that my parishioners were perhaps more stressed about their jobs than about their diseases. I, quite frankly, was not a woke pastor where far too many stories of workplace loneliness were concerned.

I had simply overlooked the message of Ecclesiastes 4:7-10.

I had missed an opportunity to redeem Gethsemane, especially for the lonely worker who amidst those "they're going" times could've used prayer to face temptations to change jobs, quit working, or more commonly stay around until some eventual retirement day.

More recently in my own retirement years, I decided to offer my still active State credentials in mental health counseling in order to help a global tele-counseling group. I did this specifically in response to the Covid-19 pandemic that was triggering depression and anxiety on a scale greater than ever before. Suicides were a daily occurrence, and I could no longer watch from the sidelines.

To my own dismay, I still hear daily in this work from individuals near and far who are suffering through the worst loneliness of their lives during this current Pandemic. Often this loneliness relates to issues within their unstable workplace. Some have felt the pain of isolation from colleagues while working from home, some the acute anxieties that come from threatened layoffs and loss of income, young adults having to move back home to their parents begging for financial survival; others trapped in dead-end jobs with little recourse for change.

One belonging to that last category is a young man I'll call Jake.

Jake came from a Christian family that moved frequently due to his father's profession as a Chaplain officer in the US Navy. The younger of two sons, Jake noted that his older brother has been determined to put down roots and stay in one place forever, while he prefers following in his father's footsteps and moving around in order to "see the world."

After graduating college in 2017 from a State university with a B.A. degree in Anthropology, he found work making or delivering pizza as his only source of income for paying basic bills. He had no money for graduate studies as needed for his career goals, and he couldn't locate any meaningful work commensurate with his Bachelor's level expertise. Yet, he had a burning desire to **"help people better themselves"** in some capacity. Finally, near the end of 2018, he was hired to work with a 2-year contract to teach English to children in China. He landed in a most unfamiliar setting within the larger coastal city of Shantou and joined a staff that had no other Americans. The other English teachers on site were from England, Australia, or South Africa. They had formed their own cliques, and he was the lone American both in his immediate workgroup and his building complex.

Jake had no prior teaching experience of any kind, nor any training in childhood development or even linguistics. He was tasked immediately with teaching as many as 240 Chinese students each week ranging in age from 2-18. His responsibility is to provide 16 grade levels of English language instruction, which requires 16 daily lesson plans and weekly grading of 240 test papers. Classes run 6 days a week and he is expected to interact with the parents of his 240 students as well, even though he faces several language barriers (*"I've learned enough of their words to survive, and that's about it"*). Twice a week he works 12-hour days and in the summer all 6 workdays are 12 hours long. He explains, *"for every school day a child misses, he must make up that day during the summer months and so the classrooms are full morning to night every summer."*

Now Jake confides in me saying *"I hate my job,"* yet he remains under contract not only for the 2-year term that would have ended with this calendar year but for a minimum of six more months due to the travel restrictions imposed by Covid-19. He laments that *"this was to be the year I would at least get to travel to new places and see the sites since the first year I was just saving up money for that purpose. Now I can't really go anyplace outside my own city."* Were he to quit his job and seek to travel home, reaching the United States would *"take a month of waiting for a flight and cost a fortune I don't have."*

After shopping his resume with countless US employers who have no interest in his level of education and experience as expressed in endless rejections or non-replies, Jake would easily resonate with the writer of Ecclesiastes: **This also is vanity and an unhappy business.**

In his own experience of vanity amidst his toil, Jake found himself seeking ways that he might commit suicide. He noted that his patience with even the least disappointment had worn so thin that he would notice himself uncharacteristically losing his temper even with his own pupils, after which he would feel very guilty. He had no one to talk to who could speak English and possibly identify with his sense of both loneliness and futility. He felt hopeless.

When I asked about Jake's Christian faith and any church background, noting his father's service as a retired Navy Chaplain, he pointed out that his church back home in the States had dropped all contact with him upon his graduation from the state university. *"While in college, I would hear from them sometimes. Newsletters, cards, things like that. I'd go home for holidays and they'd all recognize me like on Christmas and stuff. But when I moved away, my parents said they gave the church office my address here in China. I've never heard from them, though. Not anyone in the congregation. Not an email or anything."*

Then I decided to ask a follow-up question.

Would you be willing to contact your church back home in the US and let them know you could use some prayers and some friendly correspondence for a change?

Jake's answer troubles me immensely. He had only this in way of an answer to my question: *"No, it wouldn't matter. They still wouldn't do anything about it. They don't really care, and I don't either at this point. I've just moved on."*

It troubles me to think that there are probably many Jakes among the increasing number of young Americans, many with similar aspirations of being able to **"help people better themselves,"** lonely in their quest for work fulfillment, and who's religious affiliation is now "none" or "done." I wonder how many have, like Jake, "just moved on." Maybe never to return after the church community was missing in action during their own age of loneliness. Those like Jake who have been tempted to give up when far from home and feeling mentally and emotionally exhausted from their labors are living life in a churchless Gethsemane. They are sweating blood, as it were, while their church lies asleep.

The marketplace for those disciples of Jesus today who would learn from their own mistake, like my own, as well as that of those original disciples who slept at the edges of Gethsemane that night, is surely ripe with opportunity. It exists wherever bad news is heard, seen, and felt by anyone while alone. Even while in the utter loneliness of a workplace when tempted to just put in the time and wait for the weekend. Or for the retirement check.

The good news the church is tasked with sharing has no fertile soil except where bad news is already leading us into temptation. Even that writer of Ecclesiastes, perhaps the worst "bad news" book in the entire Bible, after accounting for all the reasons to give up on life like Jake nearly did, ends his account of vanities with good news. As Eugene Peterson's **"The Message"**

puts it, the last word involves the God of all good news who will eventually ***bring everything that we do out into the open and judge it according to its hidden intent, whether it's good or evil (***Ecclesiastes 12:14)**.** More often than not what we do is done with good intent, and even better results than we're even aware of.

If only Jake's church had been awake and aware enough to share their good news. Enough to have noted even his good intention, career goal, and life mission, **"help people better themselves,"** is in the open for God to judge and appreciate, even when he alone could not see the good. His teaching of English to as many as 240 Chinese children is not in vain. It is the very fulfillment of his life mission! His workplace burnout means he has gotten weary in well doing. Even while toiling seemingly alone in his own garden of Gethsemane.

Chapter 5

There is a word that is not often on our lips as Christians but may live somewhere in our heart of hearts. That word is "assimilation." For the most part it means to "blend in and conform, to join with others." It involves basic works of hospitality.

But for churches, the most unspoken yet desirable aspect of "assimilation" often goes like this: "You are welcome to come and join us, blending in and conforming with us, and doing things our way. But we have no interest or intention of going and joining you, assimilating with you, or doing things your way."

The burden of assimilation is on the outsider to come inside. We want to wear the home uniforms, as it were. You get to be on the "visitors" team.

Imagine, if you will, that the disciples of Jesus whom he invited, even entrusted, to come and pray with him, had invited Jesus in turn to instead join him as they took their naps that night at the edge of Gethsemane. Afterall, they were in the majority. Why not do things their way? They may never have done it before like Jesus was now requesting. Why not just continue their good tradition and sleep when tired? Let Jesus assimilate with them.

Churches routinely invite others to come and join with the unspoken expectation of assimilation. Churches may blindly miss the part about an outsider needing for the church to come to them and pray with them about a kind of blood, sweat, and tears crisis in that person's life. At an inconvenient time. In a strange place. Yet, this is the most opportune time and place for the church to act in way of assimilation.

Such a time and place may well be the outsider's own garden of Gethsemane loneliness.   Doing this at the beginning of a new member's relationship may be transformational within the life of the church. Starting with the hearts of the insiders.

The 10th chapter of the book of Acts reveals a transformational story within the life of the early church.  It involves the personal transformation of Simon Peter.  As a Jesus-follower extraordinaire, Peter has already gone from making a trio of mistakes near the end of Jesus's life to now becoming the church's first great evangelist.  You may recall that, as previously noted, Peter slept instead of staying awake to pray with Jesus, he drew his sword to defend Jesus (per John's account) against the will of Jesus yet again, and he later denied even being with Jesus at all.  A trifecta of human errors, to say the least.  Yet, something about the resurrected Jesus and later on the restored Holy Spirit has had a changing effect upon this remarkable disciple and now apostle.  And that's even before the story of transformation we find in Acts chapters 10.

Leading into this story, the only members of this original church of Jesus followers were Jewish.  At its onset Christianity was another sect of Judaism.  Jewish laws and customs were carefully observed, but Christ was viewed in their midst as the Jewish Messiah in fulfillment of their own prophetic tradition.

Until.

Acts 10 tells of the first Gentile converts to Christianity.  Beginning with a Roman soldier whose rank was roughly equivalent to a Master Sargent in our own Army.  He was a man of accomplished leadership named Cornelius.  Cornelius was stationed in the city of Caesarea, which was by all accounts the Roman headquarters for the region of Palestine.  And while being considered spiritual but not religious (yes, such people have long existed upon the earth), Cornelius was given to understand that he should seek out a follower of Jesus named Peter for a meeting that would take place in his house near his Caesarea army post.   His agenda was to hear what Peter had to say about this Jesus of Nazareth. Seekers always have agendas.

Having dispatched three of his men to carry this invitation to Peter, it was God's pleasure to communicate a very strange message to Peter, not once but three times. As if in a trance or a dream state, Peter could hear God telling him *"what God has made clean, you must not call profane"* (Acts 10:15). After which God communicated the message that three men would be arriving to meet him in Jerusalem and invite him to this meeting with Cornelius up in Caesarea, some distance away.

The significance of this story up to this point is that Peter would have never agreed to go with anyone to meet with a Gentile individual in a Gentile home inside a Gentile community. For any reason! Why not? Because such people and homes were unclean, profane and, well, un-Jewish. Yet, Peter had now been told that *"what God has made clean, you must not call profane."*

Strange.

Now here was Peter going with these three Gentiles to this home of essentially an enemy of his own people, a soldier of significant rank within the occupation Army carrying out martial law against Peter's own people, the Jews of Palestine. That's what I mean about transformation. As I said earlier, something about the resurrected Jesus and later on the restored Holy Spirit moved Simon Peter from where he once was to where he now is within the story of Acts 10.

The story continues with Peter and six other Jews he takes with him to Caesarea, where Cornelius played host with a group of his own friends and family to hear Peter's testimony to his faith in the risen Christ and in the power of God's Holy Spirit. As part of that testimony, Peter shared how God had communicated to him that *"what God has made clean, you must not call profane."* Cornelius then testified in like manner how God had communicated to him the need to send for Peter to hear what he would have to say about Jesus.

Beyond coincidence!

Before the meeting was over, these gathered Gentiles were replicating the very scene of Pentecost when the gathered Jews received the power of God's Holy Spirit by being able to speak in tongues. After which the Gentiles were baptized as converts to faith in Jesus and in his full baptism. Bottom line, these Roman Gentiles had now joined the original church of Jesus Christ.

I told you it was strange.

From Acts chapter 10 on, Christianity became an inclusive and global faith for Jews and Gentiles alike after the examples of Peter and Cornelius. Opening the door to Paul's own missionary journeys.

So why do I share this story now? In this current chapter? And around the question of "assimilation" and the joining that happens between the church and those professing faith in the baptized Jesus Christ, crucified and resurrected? Because this story highlights the process by which such joining and assimilation happens when God's Spirit is in the lead and we as the church are following.

Notice two particulars from this critical story in church history.

First, it wasn't that the early church had to first go out looking for Gentiles to convert to their own cause. Just because Gentiles may not have been religious in any formal or organized way did not mean they were not spiritual. God's prevenient grace was evidenced by the Holy Spirit's work within Cornelius prior to his having even met this Jesus-following churchman named Peter. This wasn't about the church staying inside because they needed to sell or get rid of what they had. This was about the church going outside because they had what they could get rid of.

There's a profound difference here, if you'll permit my little sidebar of a point to be made.

Getting rid of what we have in life is called "selling" but having what we can get rid of (what others are needing and wanting) is called "marketing." Subtle, perhaps, but nevertheless true. Many churches even today are known for what they sell. Anything from cabbage rolls to used children's' clothing and in between are sold inside church basements and fellowship halls. And with these sales comes the not-so-subtle message, **"come and join us."** We have things to get rid of and we need all the help we can get, so long as you're willing to assimilate and do things our way. All the way down to the order of worship and the selection of our own liturgies. And other rules having to do with things like food. Friendly churches everywhere are staying inside and welcoming the stranger who comes forth to join and assimilate. Even if that word, "assimilation," is rarely spoken. It is often at the very heart of church evangelism and, uh, fundraising.

Now for the second point about this critical history of Peter's visit to Cornelius.

This was not a sales call where Peter and his 6 cohorts of fellow Jews looked on from outside the front door as Peter displayed his wares and invited Cornelius to sign on the bottom line. No pitch about scheduling their trip down to Jerusalem to get baptized, join the church, and pledge a tithe to the annual budget as new members in good standing before God and God's people. Rather this was Peter and his fellow Jews going inside and essentially joining the Gentiles and following their norms and customs and assimilating into their culture for that occasion. What came from that, according to Acts 10:48, was an invitation to stay on at the home of this Roman soldier for several more days.

Talk about transformation.

Even today, this isn't how it works in most churches. Not even close.

Want to be baptized? You come to us and we'll figure out a time for your baptism in the presence of our people. Bring your people along. We relish their attendance. You can then join the church on our terms and assimilate yourselves into our rituals and conform to our standards of membership. We don't go and stay with you for several days. You come and study with us and fellowship with us for several days. Or weeks. And when you're good and ready to become like us, we'll offer you a spot on some ministry team.

All of which makes the story of Peter and six of his Jewish believers so very powerful when it comes to the issue of "assimilation."

Years ago, in my own practice as a marital and family therapist, I studied for two years under a training program in what was called Structural and Strategic Family Therapy. Much of it was based on the theory and practice of that renowned Argentinian Psychiatrist, Salvador Minuchin, M.D. In this program Dr. Minuchin's practical techniques were informed by two essential theories. They made up his core beliefs. The first was that no therapist could ever influence a family in any positive, healing way without helping to restructure and reorganize themselves for the solving of their own presenting problem. Minuchin believed that every family had a structural foundation around which they were organized to solve family problems. As in all social organizations, roles are assumed, and rules are followed. When new problems or "crises" occur, old structures fail. Protections break down. And the family roles and rules become dysfunctional. The therapist's role at such a point involved helping the family unit get restructured and re-organized to take on this new problem or "crisis" their old roles and rules had failed to prepare them for.

Now for the second of Minuchin's core beliefs or "practical theories" of family counseling.

No therapist could ever help to restructure or reorganize any family along more functional lines until she or he had first joined with the family by accommodating and "assimilating" into their own family rules and rituals. Asking the family member who had first reached out for help such questions as "how do you do things and when do you do them in this family?" became a kind of therapeutic beginning point. No different than Peter joining the Gentiles in the home of their spokesperson, Cornelius, to find out what his own agenda was so he could play by their own house-rules. Rules no longer profane in God's presence.

Want to influence people who are different? Want to challenge and help them to live their own best life story moving forward? Then start by joining them. Assimilating with them and conforming to their rules. Rules no longer profane in God's presence.

It's what a "woke" church does.

It's how that church stays awake and prays with Jesus when, upon his new crisis, he finds himself in the unlikely garden of Gethsemane and seeking the church's support. It's how that church travels from Jerusalem to Caesarea to join a Gentile family in the unlikely home of a Roman soldier named Cornelius. It's how the woke church redeems Gethsemane.

Unfortunately, that too often fails to happen.

Take the case of a lady I will call Josephine. Or make that Jo, for short. For the past three years Jo has lived alone in a generally quiet Minneapolis neighborhood, a retired schoolteacher who is widowed and her children all grown. Jo is African-American, but her neighborhood is racially mixed and so when she sought out a nearby Protestant Church she could actually walk to, she went expecting to find what would amount to the same mix of members from her own neighborhood.

That is what Jo was seeking and expecting.

What she found was a rather different matter.  It was a lovely group of white (with two or three exceptions) folks, all of whom were very nice and cordial.  Most went out of their way to welcome Jo upon her very first visit.  Would she like a bulletin? Would she like to sit here? Would she like to share a hymnal?  Would she like a cup of coffee following the service?  Would she like a free loaf of bread, and maybe some free literature, to take home with her?  Would she like to come back next Sunday and sit in on their adult Sunday School class?

Jo felt altogether welcomed into this church from her very first visit.  She even met another retired teacher in their midst, attending that adult Sunday School class she agreed to visit.  And before she knew it, she was being invited to meet other folks who had things in common with her and new friendships were formed.

Over the next couple years or so, Jo found herself immersed in the life of her new church.  But by far her closest friendships were developed within the Altar Guild she joined.  Together with the other ladies serving with her, she formed lasting friendships around the common interest in preparing the sanctuary altar and its surrounding chancel with visual appeal for the worship space each week throughout the year.  She was able to use her skills as a former Art teacher and received high praise from her pastor and colleagues in volunteer ministry.

No one made an issue of race during the years Jo had served within her church, even though she was the lone African-American in the Guild and the pastoral staff included two white men and one white woman.  Race was mostly an after-thought.

At least that was so until May 25, 2020.

What happened that day rocked the entire community in which Jo and her church were located in Minneapolis.

It was on that day that another African-American, George Floyd, was murdered at 38th St. and Chicago Avenue by a team of Minneapolis police officers. This act was so brutal as to trigger an outpouring of shock and sympathy, as well as rage, across the nation and literally around the world. Protest marches sprang up in Minneapolis, and also in cities around the globe. Rioting occurred on streets adjacent to the protests. Smoke from these riots was visible, even breathable, from the neighborhood church Jo so loved.

This past September, Jo reflected upon her experiences over the summer as she wrote these words to me in an email, **"Coach Rivers was exactly right when he said, 'It's amazing why we keep loving this country, and this country does not love us back.' That's exactly how I'm now feeling about this church I belong to."**

How so? I wanted to know so I quickly replied back to her. What happened at church that you're feeling unloved?

Immediately, Jo returned my reply.

She explained that while they'd been meeting in virtual church via YouTube each week for worship due to the COVID-19 Pandemic, she and her Guild (Jo now chaired the Altar Guild) colleagues had been faithfully preparing the Altar each week for worship as before in order to make visible the colors and décor needed to accentuate the camera-eye view of each service. She met with her pastor and colleagues each week via Zoom. A few days following Mr. Floyd's death, they had a meeting in which Jo expressed the depth of her own heartache and the personal sense of grief she was experiencing. No one responded. She went on to tell them that tomorrow's protest march was one she would be attending, **"and would anyone else like to come along. I reassured them we would all be safe together."** She was speaking about the planned protest marching from the State Capital building in neighboring St. Paul going to the Governor's residence that next day on June 1st. Excuses were raised. No one else was able to go with her.

Or willing?

*"Nor,"* Joe continued in her email, *"did any of them, not a one, even bother to pick the phone up to call me that next evening to see how it went. Nor text me. No emails. Nothing!!! Not the pastor. Not a single member of our Guild. Not a soul anywhere else in that church did anything to participate in the protest with me. So, I kept going back every day for a week and joining the protests just on my own."*

What struck me the most in reading Jo's expressed account of her experiences is that even though she mentioned feelings of appreciation for the other protestors, white and black, young and old, and *"even some other clergy from other churches……"* the absence of her own church family from such events left her with a kind of loneliness that was soon to approach even bitterness. And, hence, her echo of the Doc Rivers quote, *"…… 'It's amazing why we keep loving this country, and this country does not love us back.' That's exactly how I'm now feeling about this church I belong to."*

So, what, again, is the issue here?

Is it not the question of what happens when "assimilation" requires conformity on the member's part upon joining the church instead of the church's part on joining the member?

To be fair, there is no perfect church. No church exists that will not step on some sore toes among its varied members. But sensitivity to felt needs and sought for agendas isn't the standard that makes up a "woke" church. All of us are insensitive and ill equipped to read minds or, for that matter, conform to the expectations of every member.

What a "woke" church does best is what Peter did best in relation to Cornelius and the Gentiles. Such a church eliminates all barriers of profanity, understanding that *"what God has made clean, you must not*

***call profane.***" And instead of saying, in effect, *"no, we can't come to you. You come to us,"* the woke church is one that makes joining and "assimilation" truly a two-way street. Or as Dr. Minuchin used to say, *"you can't help them until you join them."* Especially in their own age of loneliness; their personal garden of Gethsemane.

Today's unsolved problem of fatal police assaults against unarmed African Americans is going to require community restructuring and reorganizing. The old roles and rules are not working. Like families, communities can become dysfunctional. Those like Jo who invite the church to come and help are too often like Jesus in the garden of Gethsemane.

If only the church today would learn the lesson of Acts 10 and act like Peter. If only today's church would better practice effective "assimilation." If only today's church would redeem Gethsemane.

*PART TWO*         *"Signs of Redemption"*

*Then the righteous will answer him, 'Lord, when was it that we saw you hungry and gave you food, or thirsty and gave you something to drink? And when was it that we saw you a stranger and welcomed you, or naked and gave you clothing? And when was it that we saw you sick or in prison and visited you?' And the king will answer them, 'Truly I tell you, just as you did it to one of the least of these who are members of my family, you did it to me.' -- Jesus Christ (Matthew 25:37-40)*

Chapter 6

One of the key ways of distinguishing a woke church from its alternative may best be found in the biblical story of Martha and Mary, sisters who both loved Jesus but in very distinctive ways. The story is found in Luke 10:38-42, and it goes like this:

*Now as they went on their way, he (Jesus) entered a certain village, where a woman named Martha welcomed him into her home. She had a sister named Mary, who sat at the Lord's feet and listened to what he was saying. But Martha was distracted by her many tasks; so, she came to him and asked, "Lord, do you not care that my sister has left me to do all the work by myself? Tell her then to help me." But the Lord answered her, "Martha, Martha, you are worried and distracted by many things; there is need of only one thing. Mary has chosen the better part, which will not be taken away from her."*

A Martha church is focused on doing all the things right. A Mary church is focused on doing all the right things.

A woke church, upon which Gethsemane's redemption depends, is more like Mary in this story.

I learned of this important distinction when talking recently to a friend of mine who teaches at a Church of God seminary in our neighboring state of Indiana. Her name is Sarah, and she vividly recalls a time in her life when she was more like Martha herself. She was in the early years of her own seminary studies, prior to receiving her D.Min. She had relocated from out of state and was trying to find her way in a new community that included joining a new church. This was in line with her academic requirements. However, at her rather young age she was somewhat intimidated by the members of this church, who seemingly emphasized propriety and professionalism at every turn. It was a congregation that exuded perfectionism in all of its activities, starting with the worship experience. Every "t" was crossed, every "i" dotted. No room for error.

And never was this more so than in the choir loft, where Sarah was one of the strong voiced "first sopranos." Every introit, extroit, and anthem was sung without blemish.

Some churches seem to any such observer as if they have it "all together." What, then, happens to these observers when they hit a rough patch in their own personal life in which they don't have it anywhere close to all together? Sarah was one such observer. She did hit such a rough patch. And she didn't have it all together.

Sarah relates in her own story of how throughout her life she was made to feel different because of a slew of different medical issues she had to face. She had wanted nothing more than to "fit in" and be like everyone else. Everyone else who seemingly had it all together. And so, when the time came for her to face a life-threatening surgery to remove potentially malignant polyps near her brain that had caused her debilitating headaches in recent months, she decided it would be her fate to bear this burden alone lest others in church think less of her. Rather than appear vulnerable, Sarah would remain stoic in the church's presence. Calm as a duck above the water's surface; all the while paddling like crazy underneath where others could not see.

The problem with belonging to a church where nobody knows you is that nobody then appears to care. And like many a good member belonging to what amounts to a Martha church, everything is about appearances and no one dares reveal their rough edges for others' inspection. The social norm in a Martha church where some sister Mary dares to have rough edges is that Jesus gets an earful along the lines of **"Lord, do you not care that my sister has left me to do all the work by myself? Tell her then to help me."**

Sarah's story is all the more compelling because she is a member of something larger than the church in our contemporary society. She belongs to the millennial generation. The generation that carries about its own unique norms, perhaps the first one being: Be authentic. Appear as yourself, and not as someone else wants you to look, sound, or act.

Because Sarah's life-vocation was to involve church pastoral ministry (eventually as a seminary professor in training future pastors), she did not leave the church despite questions of whether her own authenticity would even be tolerated. Many in her generation do just that, and Sarah might otherwise have been one of them.

What instead happened is that Sarah dared to be transparent and reveal her own vulnerability…her roughest of edges…. telling her choir that she was facing a life-threatening surgery and needed them to pray with her lest she be tempted to postpone or cancel it all. Without her realizing it at the time, this was to be a test of whether hers was a Martha church or a Mary church. She refused to simply assume the former, despite all other signs pointing in that direction.

I find myself wondering if Sarah wasn't up to such a risk many millennials would back out of because, unlike so many others her own age, Sarah had already faced one medical and surgical risk after another throughout her lifetime. She was a consummate risk taker, perhaps more than she was a new seminarian who by calling felt obligated to grant the church several second chances to behave with transparent authenticity for a change.

Want to know what happened?

On the evening prior to her "next day surgery," Sarah was sitting at home alone. Praying in her own lonely garden of Gethsemane. Tempted to maybe still postpone the next day's risky surgery to remove these polyps near her brain. No sign of her choir or any other part of her church family's presence.

Until.

The phone rang. It was Alycia. The lady who sat next to her in choir. She called to announce she would like to come over for a bit just to have prayer with her. Now. This evening. In just a few minutes she would be there. There inside Sarah's cramped and cluttered little apartment.

Sarah's first reply was "yes" but her second thought was "oh, no, my place is a wreck." No time to vacuum the cat hair off the sofa. No time to pack away any clutter into the other closet. No way to get ready for this possible "Martha-type," who would soon see that her place was not in perfect order.

Have you ever been there? I mean, in Sarah's shoes, wondering how your own church might judge you if someone were to see cat hair or anything else maybe out of place on your sofa? If so, you may belong to a Martha church. Or you may even be a Martha yourself.

Martha was so worried about what Jesus would think of her place that she couldn't stop working to have everything prepared to a tee for his visit. Judging her sister as wrong to care somehow only about being with Jesus, and not about impressing him with nice appearances and smooth edges. Surely Jesus would condemn any dirty appearance and rough edge.

Right?

Wrong!

Jesus couldn't have cared less about what Martha's place looked like. He was coming to be with them in supportive friendship and nothing else. He was all about transparent authenticity, much like today's church-avoiding millennial generation

Sarah continues with her story. She tells me about how Alycia came over and sat, yes, right on that same sofa that still had the cat hair on it. Had to maybe move a few newspapers or even textbooks in order to make a place for herself to sit down. But there she was. Entering Sarah's own garden of Gethsemane. Praying with her about the temptation to just "let this cup just pass" from Sarah. Or not. Praying for Sarah's courage to go through with tomorrow's surgery. For her strength. For the resurrection that could possibly come about for her after a successful surgery bringing an end to her debilitating headaches. They prayed together, and not alone. And, as Sarah went on to explain to me, it made all the difference in the world.

Sarah did go through with the high-risk surgery she'd been tempted to cancel at the last minute. And good news! The polyps were removed, they were not malignant, and she did recover (resurrection!) without the debilitating headaches.

It was this experience of a woke church member, visiting her in a less than clean or straightened up apartment but in her own age of loneliness, that connected Sarah to her church as never before. And revealed her church to be everything that she, and Jesus, hoped it would be.

A Mary church.

A church where doing right things topped doing things right. A church where Gethsemane is redeemed. And where the least of these are treated like Christ himself thanks to those like Mary, and a first soprano named Alycia, who chose the better part.

Chapter 7

A very new friend of mine whom I will call "Pat" offers up a story of her own redemption.  She preferred not to write anything down but to instead talk by phone about what it was like being herself both outside and inside the church.  I found out in a hurry that Pat loves to talk.  But in a good way.

First her outsider story.

Pat grew up in a family of sisters but playing the strange part of her daddy's lone "tomboy."  She was the middle daughter of 5 girls, no boys.  As I listened to her story, I could only imagine what it may have felt like coming in the door in "overalls," as she called them, and getting washed up for the dinner after returning home with her father from a long day of hauling beef cattle out in west Texas.  Dad had his own 18-wheeler rig with cattle trailer.  That was his livelihood.  Transporting cows from pen to market to pen and back again.

She was her father's favorite because she alone among the 5 daughters wanted to ride along on those non-school days when he would leave home at 5 a.m. for the long run to load up and down the mostly rural highways of their Lone Star state.  She grew up answering to the labels of cowgirl and tomboy without complaint.  Or almost no complaining, except in relation to her prettier, more petite, and far more feminine sisters.  To say that she fit in among the rest of the girls at home, or even in the rest of the coeds at school, would be a far stretch.  She describes hating the rare but still present occasions as a youngster having to wear a "girl's dress," as it felt so out of place on her own more rugged physique. The strange thing she'd wanted most growing up, she tells me, was to have been born a boy instead of a girl.

Pat described for me a highlight of her school days. While in the 11th grade, she made history at least in her part of the state by being the first ever girl to make the boy's high school football team, teeing up as the Bulldog's place-kicker to start the game or at least the second half. Extra points and field goals were her thing. Better than the other boys who tried out for that position. And running out onto the gridiron on those west Texas Friday nights with all the guys made her feel like something of a celebrity.

However, when it came time to run off the field after the final seconds of the clock at the corner of that end zone ticked their way into a Bulldog victory, or the even the rare defeat, she would not leave with the team for its own team locker room. Her post-game departure would be to her own "girl's restroom" in whatever school building they would be using. There she would incur the stares of other girls coming in together, leaving together, and whispering about her as they left.

Loneliness.

Why, she wondered, did she have to be so different from the other girls? And the other boys? Why did the defeats feel so defeating after her high school football games, especially if she had the misfortune of missing a critical field goal or extra point? And why did even the victories feel so shallow, even if she had kicked the winning score? Why had God made her so, well, different?

Indeed, that is what Pat often asked herself and even God while bouncing along those long prairie highways in the passenger seat of her Dad's semi, rocking as it did with a trailer full of less-than-contented cows shifting back and then forth. All as that man she called daddy strong-armed the steering wheel to correct for the hard pull of their trailer. Yet, he loved having her along for the ride and made it a point to introduce her to the gear shift she would learn long before getting a Texas Intermediate driver's license on her 16th birthday. She learned to watch for truck mph and engine rpm while then handling the gear shift and splitter moving it down, across, up and again down through most of its 18 different speeds. Daddy taught her about how trailer loads, and road conditions effected the overall use of those speeds. Yet, for all the pleasure she found in helping him on the truck, there was no one else at home to tell. No one else cared about what pleasure she had either on the truck with daddy or the team with the Bulldogs on those Fall Friday nights. Who could she tell about the things she enjoyed the most in her young life? Well, no one, really, as she reminisced in my presence.

Loneliness.

Even Pat's daddy was not much for sports and had no real interest in her role as a placekicker on the high school team. Mom was busy working with her four sisters, none of them really caring to know what Pat was going through in her times of travel or times of victory or, especially, those bitter nights of gridiron defeat. Nor could her football teammates really find anything at all in common with Pat's stories of the open road, hauling steers up and down and criss-cross between western and northern cattle barns in their Lone Star state.

No wonder Pat often felt like a lone star, though certainly not starlet, within her own adolescent identity of "differentness."

Perhaps to no one's surprise, graduation from high school and then her 18th birthday to follow meant the day had finally arrived when Pat could study for her own CDL (commercial driver's license) in the State of Texas, enabling her to take the wheel of the family-owned rig and show her dad that she had absorbed many of his lessons growing up in that cab's well-broken in passenger seat throughout the holiday breaks and then summer months leading up to football practices every August. With this it was time to discard the two or three skirts and blouses, or at least skirts and, for sure, both dresses that still hung in her closet back home. From now on, jeans and western shirts were the order of the day, the only attire she is needing in her now adult wardrobe.

So where was the church that Pat grew up attending there in her small-town Texas community? Did she still attend with the rest of her family? These are questions I hoped she could answer one way or the other, as she related what it was like being the "only one" like her during those formative years of identity crises through which we all, at some point, must "find ourselves."

*"Do you want to know the truth?"* Pat answered when I pressed her to describe what it was like being her own unique and sometimes lonely self also where her Baptist Church was concerned growing up. In her own words, *"For me the best part was the church dinners. I went to a place where all the women were good cooks. No, make that great cooks, and it seemed like about every month or so there'd be a big meal of some kind served down in the church basement where we'd go through the line and help yourself to all kinds of different fried chicken, pot roast, ham, sweet potato casseroles, and about anything else a growing kid could ever be hungry for, pies or cakes or cookies or you name it."* Her family never missed a church dinner, even if they sometimes found different excuses for not always showing up for worship on Sunday mornings. And, yes, she did have to attend Sunday School with the rest of the kids growing up, and vacation Bible school and all that. She was baptized as a 10-year-old, as best she could recall, and did like playing games with the other kids at church. Mostly played during youth group up through high school. After that, however, it was hard for Pat to get herself up in time for church on Sundays. The adult Sunday School classes were worse than boring, and most kids her age skipped any activity going on at church soon as they graduated, even if they stayed there in town for work or Community College.

One thing that stayed the same for Pat after high school was that even as she helped her Dad with his trucking business during the week, Sundays were the day to rest. Watch football. Or maybe work on her own car she was able to buy with money saved up from high school graduation gifts, birthdays, and whatever Dad thought her help was worth to him as a kind of "hired hand" in working with the cattle for transport while loading, unloading, and of course, now driving.  Her ability to tinker with her car's various parts and mechanical features came from those times on the road when, as she explained, *"my daddy used to open up the hood and send me for the toolbox whenever we'd need to work together on that baby's front end."*  Or trailer, for that matter.  *"That's what the overalls were for, some days we had to get a little grease and dirt under our fingernails.  Went with the territory."*

And loneliness?   Did you ever still feel that?

Well, yes, Pat responded.  There was still some of that.  Especially on Saturday nights.  Nothing really to do in their small town, and no one to do it with.  Even her younger, prettier, sisters were going out on dates already.  Mostly, Pat found herself staying home with the folks.  Going to bed early.  Playing cards with her daddy, usually Gin Rummy, or sometimes Spades.  Mom didn't care to join in very often.  And no one else but her cared much for sports on TV.  The occasional rodeo in town, especially during County Fair week, brought the whole family out of the house, usually together.  *"But, yes,"* she answered, *"there was still lonely times after I graduated high school."*

And the church, I persisted.   Did they make things better or worse during that particular age of loneliness?

*"Well, eventually they did make it better.  Much better, in fact."*  How so?  By giving her a job driving a church bus on Sunday mornings to pick up kids for Sunday School sometime after her 21st birthday.  Taking advantage of her CDL and ability to handle the demands of driving precious cargo, especially those sweet little kids that came each week full of anticipation and then returned after church with hands and laps and pockets full of special handmade objects used for remembering Bible verses and all.  It was a chance for Pat to join in the Education ministry of her congregation and be part of helping others find meaning and joy in their own lives.  Even to the point of being able to spot those lonely kids on the bus that had no one, not even a family, to join with and who would

be sitting alone with little attention drawn from other kids there on the bus. She knew which kids lived with single Moms, which kids lived even with grandparents and without any siblings, or which kids just stood out as being, well, outcasts in their own little worlds of loneliness. They were the ones Pat paid special attention to each week, reminding them they were welcome aboard and lovingly attended to while in her care riding back and forth to their Sunday School class or Vacation Bible School.

Should the old school buses need extra mechanical attention after their Sunday runs, Pat was someone the church learned to depend on for help. By now she had her own toolbox behind the seat of her **"used Chevy Tundra"** pickup truck. She was as good of mechanic as the church had to turn to, even though their fleet of 6 buses were used to routine shop maintenance twice a year down at a local garage. Seemed like there was always something needing tweaked or repaired here and there throughout the year. Not worth an extra trip down to the garage. Pat's chance to give back to the church, and to feel needed and helpful. Less lonely.

Then there was the day Pat got a call from the church to see if she'd be willing to serve on their Building and Grounds Committee. Helping to oversee all of the church property, and not just the Sunday School buses. Why not, she thought. She could do that. Sure, it would mean arranging her truck-driving schedule such that she would be home the second Tuesday of every month by 7 p.m. for Committee. And Saturday's were often given over to Committee work for the church, as well. But they needed her. And she was more than capable of helping the guys, as it turned out, decide what needed doing and where and when. And how.

By the time Pat was ready to celebrate her 30th birthday, still living at home with Mom and Dad, her sisters "all married off," she was not only still on the Building and Grounds Committee, but now the elected "Chairman." Technically, their "Chairwoman." All in a church that didn't take kindly as a rule to women in authority. Yet, Pat was different, in a good way. They counted on her skills in operating the work of this Committee of otherwise good old boys from west Texas who needed someone to take charge and tell them what tonight's agenda was, what needed fixing and when and how and such. She was it. Chairwoman of the Building and Grounds Committee. First, one year. And then the next. And by now 6 years had gone by when I was able to talk to Pat about how the church was there for her, with her, to cross out any of what might otherwise have been for her the loneliness of Gethsemane.

Yes, Pat was still living at home. Yes, her Dad was now making fewer and fewer trips with her on the truck. Yes, it was now her trucking business to manage, her loads to bid on and secure for their little family company. Her name on all the contracts, all the equipment leases, and her co-signature on any deals she and Dad were making over the course of every workweek. Dad was gradually giving her more and more responsibility for the day-to-day operation. And, like her role as Chair of the church committee despite her being a woman, she was the daughter Dad most counted on to make sure the whole family got along together. Everybody having what they needed to get by. You might as well say the family hero or heroine. Vehicles all running. Supplies all ordered. Bills all paid. When it was time to "git er done," it was Pat everyone could count on to take charge. To keep things running smoothly.

All with little, if any, time for loneliness. In fact, far less than Pat had ever known while raised as that family "tomboy and cowgirl" growing up with **"no one to tell"** after all those rides, and those close scores in her Bulldog football uniforms, as a lonely teenager in small town America. Thank God for the church that was there with her when it counted the most, and for Pat when they needed her the most later on. And for the men in her "woke" church. Thankfully, they were not the least bit intimidated by a strong younger woman whose take-charge reliability was just what they needed. Pat was their problem-solver in overalls. Finally, Pat had a place to belong. At church she felt like "one of the guys."

The Old Testament book of Judges contains a host of different stories having to do with problem-solving within God's larger economy. Throughout the Bible we read of human problems matched up with Godly solutions sent mostly through persons of unique distinction. Some were, quite obviously, more unique than others. God was an equal-opportunity recruiter and supplier where the task of earthly problem-solving was concerned.

Long before any Christian Apostles ever admonished women to remain silent and submissive to any sort of cultural patriarchy, God rose up a prophet in the land of Israel named Deborah. She became Judge over all of Israel in the 12$^{th}$ Century BC. The "woke" people of Israel were not intimidated by a strong younger woman whose take-charge reliability would be the problem-solver they needed.

To admit that Deborah was different, perhaps even to the extent that "loneliness" was a never-ending thorn in her flesh, is to state the obvious. None of Israel's other Judges was female. None of the others actually administered Justice itself or served initially in the role of prophet. Women prophets were scarce throughout Israel, to be sure. Yet, as we read of Judge Deborah in Judges 4-5 (one chapter each telling her story in prose and then poetry), we find Deborah doing as all other Judges did: commanding armed soldiers, who just happened to all be men, and their General named Barak, also male, in the matter of Israel's public enemy #1. Jabin. King Jabin, of the Canaanite city of Hazor, whom we're told in 4:3 *"had nine hundred chariots of iron and had oppressed the Israelites cruelly twenty years."*

Speaking for God as both prophet and Judge, Deborah assigns Barak the task of deploying 10,000 soldiers from his best units and to take on this problem of oppressive King Jabin and his favorite military commander, Sisera. It was time to provide justice (God's solution) for Israel in response to the injustice (Israel's problem) of this Canaanite King. Barak, as what we in America might compare to our "Chairman of the Joint Chiefs of Staff" at our Pentagon, may not have been accustomed to taking assignments from women commanders in chief. Nor was he unaware that he would, per ancient custom, have to lead the charge against what amounted to a superior enemy army. I'm guessing Jabin's and Sisera's 900 chariots of iron stirred fears of outright mutiny in Barak's own ranks, if nothing else. He would have to prepare all of Israel's soldiers to possibly die for Israel instead of running off for their own safety. Such was the size of Israel's problem in the face of Canaan's King Jabin and his top General Sisera.

Here is where the story gets interesting.

***Barak said to her*** (Judge Deborah), ***"If you will go with me, I will go; but if you will not go with me, I will not go." And she said, "I will surely go with you; nevertheless, the road on which you are going will not lead to your glory, for the Lord will sell Sisera into the hand of a woman." Then Deborah got up and went with Barak to Kedesh. Barak summoned Zebulun and Naphtali to Kedesh; and ten thousand warriors went up behind him; and Deborah went up with him*** (Judges 4:8-10).

Quick quiz. How many of you now reading this assume that when Deborah says the Lord will sell Sisera into the hand of a woman, Deborah is talking about herself? As in, "take me along and I will take the credit for the final victory." Is Judge Deborah about to be the solution to the problem of Israel's unjust oppression beneath the armed threat posed by Sisera's King Jabin? Well, not really. Deborah doesn't care so much about claiming credit as she cares about solving the problem. And she does so by ***"the hand of a woman"*** other than herself. A woman named Jael who may never have been involved at all except for the leadership of Judge Deborah, one woman recognizing superior powers in another woman.

Let's read on a bit further.

*Jael came out to meet Sisera, and said to him, "Turn aside, my lord, turn aside to me; have no fear." So, he turned aside to her into the tent, and she covered him with a rug. Then he said to her, "Please give me a little water to drink; for I am thirsty." So, she opened a skin of milk and gave him a drink and covered him. He said to her, "Stand at the entrance of the tent, and if anybody comes and asks you, 'Is anyone here?' say, 'No.'" But Jael wife of Heber took a tent peg, and took a hammer in her hand, and went softly to him and drove the peg into his temple, until it went down into the ground—he was lying fast asleep from weariness—and he died. Then, as Barak came in pursuit of Sisera, Jael went out to meet him, and said to him, "Come, and I will show you the man whom you are seeking." So, he went into her tent; and there was Sisera lying dead, with the tent peg in his temple.*

It was Jael, you see, who ended up outsmarting King Jabin and his chief General Sisera, putting an end, albeit a gruesome one, to his injustice over Israel once and for all. As with all problems of injustice, their solution produces peace. Which lasted another forty years in Israel thanks to Judge Deborah's leadership.

Only a "woke" God would identify with an outsider (someone who seemed very "different" but brought the best available skills to the table for problem-solving in God's own Kingdom) who could find company in a group of men not intimidated by a strong and young woman leader. Only a "woke" Israel could employ such a leader as "Judge" Deborah to secure the peoples' peace with justice. Only a "woke" church did find redemption by joining with the likes of a "Chairwoman" Pat -- anything but silent and submissive – over the Building and Grounds Committee she still to this day refers to as "my guys."

Chapter 8

We can all learn a great deal from Jesus and the way he went about living his life here on earth.

For one thing, we can learn from him the best way to read the Scriptures upon which our faith is based. Jesus was the master of interpreting, understanding and applying scripture as a whole body of work, not just a verse or two here and there taken out of context. Context was everything to Jesus where reading and using his peoples' own Hebrew Bible was concerned. He looked for patterns of emphasis. Then he would apply individual verses according to similar contexts in his own time and place.

Perhaps the best example of how Jesus did this was when he gave us what we refer to as the Golden Rule and the Greatest Commandment. *"Do to others whatever you would like them to do to you. This is the essence of all that is taught in the law and the prophets"* (MT 7:12, NLT) and *"You shall love the Lord your God with all your heart, and with all your soul, and with all your mind. This is the greatest and first commandment. And a second is like it: You shall love your neighbor as yourself. On these two commandments hang all the law and the prophets"* (MT 22:37-40).

Jesus read the Hebrew Bible of his own age with an eye for the big picture patterns. Indeed, the larger context in which Matthew relates the second quote by Jesus from his 22$^{nd}$ chapter involved the Jewish sect of Sadducees. A spokesman for this sect came to Jesus with a "gotcha" verse of their own, Deuteronomy 25:5. This is a verse from a larger sermon by Moses by which the Sadducees would weaponize their argument against any belief in a resurrection or heavenly afterlife. Nor were the Sadducees alone in using the Jewish scriptures to clobber their opponents.

So, where Deuteronomy 25:5 was concerned, the Sadducees assumed they'd found a "clobber" verse (playing "gotcha") for both Jesus and the Pharisees (their opposing rivals in the faith) having to do with the resurrection. As never failed, Jesus laid low the Sadducees and their doubts about the resurrection by fully explaining DT 25:5 in its fullest and clearest context. End of contest.

Now came the Pharisees to try their own luck yet again with this same game of "gotcha" wherein they would weaponize a different verse from scripture (also from Deuteronomy 5:12 in the sacred and holy Torah). It said, **Observe the sabbath day and keep it holy, as the Lord your God commanded you.** To the Pharisees this had to be the greatest commandment, because it was the one they had perhaps the least trouble obeying. It was their "clobber" verse where their own enemies were concerned.

And now it was their chance to clobber Jesus. They asked Jesus to name the one greatest commandment in all of the Torah. So, in the larger context, this was a chance for the Pharisees to not only upstage their enemy sect, the Sadducees, but to knock Jesus off his own pedestal at the same time!

Big mistake.

In response to these Pharisees, as with the Sadducees, Jesus nixed their narrow use of a single verse for "proof texting" by broadening the biblical context and expanding the search to include Deuteronomy 6:4 and Leviticus 19:18. And not a single commandment but two Greatest commandments.

Why?

Because taken together, these two Greatest Commandments summarized the entire length and breadth of the Torah. And not only the Torah but even the writings of all the Prophets as well. They were the whole deal. Or the Holy deal.

What we learn from Jesus especially in the area of reading, understanding and applying scripture is that patterns and contexts are the keys and worthy of more frequent emphasis than the more isolated points one might at other times encounter. To miss this lesson from Jesus's life example described by the Gospelists is to miss the core pattern of our faith itself.

One such pattern we encounter in scripture has to do with caring for widows and orphans.

From the Psalmists, we read in 68:5, *"Father of the fatherless and protector of widows is God in his holy habitation."* In 82:3, *"Give justice to the weak and the fatherless; maintain the right of the afflicted and the destitute."* In 146:9, *"The Lord watches over the strangers; he upholds the orphan and the widow…."*

From the Law, we read in Exodus 22:22, *"You shall not mistreat any widow or fatherless child."* And from Deuteronomy 10:18, *"He executes justice for the fatherless and the widow, and loves the sojourner, giving him food and clothing."* In DT 14:29, **"Cursed be anyone who perverts the justice due to the sojourner, the fatherless, and the widow."** In DT 24:17, *"You shall not pervert the justice due to the sojourner or to the fatherless or take a widow's garment in pledge."* In DT 27:19, *"And the Levite, because he has no portion or inheritance with you, and the sojourner, the fatherless, and the widow, who are within your towns, shall come and eat and be filled, that the Lord your God may bless you in all the work of your hands that you do."*

From the Prophets, we have Isaiah 1:17, *"Learn to do good; seek justice, correct oppression; bring justice to the fatherless, plead the widow's cause."* Jeremiah 7:6 warns against oppressing the sojourner, the fatherless, or the widow. And again in 22:3, *"do no wrong or violence to the resident alien, the fatherless, and the widow."* Ezekiel 16:49 reminds us, *"Behold, this was the guilt of your sister Sodom: she and her daughters had pride, excess of food, and prosperous ease, but did not aid the poor and needy."* Ezekiel 22:7 goes on to explain, saying *"Father and mother are treated with contempt in you; the sojourner suffers extortion in your midst; the fatherless and the widow are wronged in you."* Zechariah 7:10 warns, *"Do not oppress the widow, the fatherless, the sojourner, or the poor, and let none of you devise evil against another in your heart."* Malachi 3:5, in turn, warns of God's judgment "…. *against those who oppress the hired worker in his wages, the widow and the fatherless, against those who thrust aside the sojourner, and do not fear me, says the Lord of hosts."*

The Apostle Paul, in his pastoral letter to young Timothy, advised that widows, especially those who were childless, were to be honored and cared for. And the New Testament Church in Jerusalem, as early as Acts 6:1, noted that *"in these days when the disciples were increasing in number, a complaint by the Hellenists arose against the Hebrews because their widows were being neglected in the daily distribution."* Without any hesitation, the Church began the practice of assigning a team of seven deacons who would handle the work of caring for the widows and all who were in need. As the Church then grew in service to those in need, many widows themselves took on a key role in caring for their own faith communities. In Acts 9:36-42 we read of one such widow, Tabitha, who was restored to life and health under the support of the other Christian widows within her port city of Joppa.

Add to that the Apostle James, who exhorts his fellow Christians writing, ***"Religion that is pure and undefiled before God, the Father, is this: to visit orphans and widows in their affliction"*** (James 1:27 ESV).

Are you seeing the broad scriptural pattern here?

The entirety of Christian scripture is covered with references to widows and orphans. These were among the loneliest, and then most often impoverished, people in the land. So little wonder that Jesus himself, never one to miss the larger scriptural forest for the isolated trees symbolizing single words or passages, picked up on the importance of honoring those who were widowed.

Luke 7:11-17 tells the story of a grieving widow in the town of Nain. Her only son had just died, or so she thought. But Jesus, full of compassion for her, tells her not to weep and tells her son to arise. As he did so, Jesus returned him to this overjoyed but still widowed mother.

Mark 12:38-44 tells the story of a time when Jesus was confronting the Hebrew Bible teachers, called Scribes, for their own negligence in the care of widows. Nearby, he called attention to a widow who was among several Jews placing offerings into the Temple treasury. In verses 41-42 we read, *"Many rich people threw in large amounts. But a poor widow came and put in two very small copper coins, worth only a fraction of a penny."*

Now listen to this.

**"Jesus said, 'I tell you the truth, this poor widow has put more into the treasury than all the others. They all gave out of their wealth; but she, out of here poverty, put in everything -- all she had to live on'"** (MK 12: 43-44). In Luke 15:8-10, Jesus relates the parable of the lost coin. Who lost it? A poor widow who needed and deeply cherished each of her coins just like God needs and deeply cherishes each one of us.

Jesus understand the scriptural mandate concerning the care of widows and orphans. His way of interpreting his own Bible we call our Old Testament was to notice the patterns and the big picture, and to not get bogged down in isolated detail or "text without context."

I mention all of this because, despite some of the progress made in at least our own culture as regards the financial support of widows and orphans, there is still a loneliness faced by these persons today that rivals anything experienced by those whom the Bible so widely referenced and honored as worthy of extra care.

This brings to mind a true story involving a friend of mine named Gary.

I first met Gary while serving as one of the pastors at the church where he and his wife, Barbara, were members here in Ohio. They had joined this church in 2006 partly due to Barbara's love of choral music, an art in which she excelled. Her voice as a first soprano was Spiritually gifted in a miraculous way that empowered her performance in various venues throughout the United States and in six other countries. More recently, Barbara sang in the chorus of our local Dayton Philharmonic Orchestra. She was a featured soloist also in a local production of Handel's Messiah. Yet, Barbara was not always welcomed by local churches in this area because to admit her was to admit her dog. Her service dog.

Barbara was blind. And her service dog was such a part of her life that, if she was to sing, her dog would be there by her side at every rehearsal and performance. No dog, no Barbara.

As I first sat down with Gary and Barbara in their home during a pastoral visit, I felt surprise in hearing that some of the other churches in our area had refused to let Barbara's dog enter their sanctuary, or their chancel and choir loft in particular. Again, it was no dog, no Barbara. No church.

In the years since that time, service dogs have become something of a popular trend. But that was not always the case, and so when our local church happened to be one that said yes to Barbara's dog in our sanctuary and even choir loft, we were blessed to have her, and Gary (and companion "Kobe" as honorary) joined into membership.

It turned out to be a rather long story as to how Barbara lost her sight.

Barbara had a most difficult childhood. She suffered repeated, traumatic child abuse growing up within her own family. Given the chance to leave home, she had gone away to college where her brilliant mind had earned her a full scholarship. Yet, it was there that her own body first began to break down, showing manifestations of prior sexual abuse in particular as she struggled with chronic bowel disease. Against a backdrop of diagnoses mixed between Chron's Disease and Ulcerative Colitis, Barbara was first prescribed a dose of Prednisone, a corticosteroid medicine, at the age of 19. With every return home to her family, her Inflammatory Bowel Disease would flare up and another dose of Prednisone would be prescribed. Given the back-and-forth changes of physicians and pharmacies over her young adulthood, it was easy for Barbara to go from one flare up to another and one period of steroid treatment after another.

Then came Gary.

Barbara's medical complications and a required hysterectomy coincided with the earlier loss of a marriage to an airman stationed at Wright Patterson Air Force Base. Gary then had the honor of coming to her rescue as she tried to recover both from divorce and hysterectomy. Barbara, in turn, rescued Gary from his own difficult and often lonely life as a single, 31-year-old airman also stationed away from home at WPAFB. Barbara desperately needed Gary at that point in her life. Gary desperately needed Barbara at that point in his life. And they joined hands in Holy Matrimony at the Base Chapel on December 5, 1980.

While serving the Air Force as a career, Gary faced a number of future assignments, including a time in Germany where Barbara, in following him, was shuttled back and forth between competing medical doctors representing different service branches with different treatment plans and overlapping prescriptions.

Little did Barbara know the toll that her corticosteroid treatments would have upon the rest of her body, including her eyesight. By the age of 38, Barbara was legally blind. And her steroid medications over the years had also led to other life-threatening infections and a complete and irreversible ileostomy.

By the time of Gary's career retirement from the Air Force, both were in agreement that the best medical care for Barbara would likely come from facilities here at Wright Patterson in Ohio. Having no children of their own and by now no parents or close family members, they clung together as two peas in a pod. They remained each other's rescuers in all matters of concern, and they were both spiritually grounded in a very deeply shared Christian faith whether in or out of any church congregation. Yet, they longed for a broader church connection to go along with their deepened-by-tragedy faith in Jesus Christ. Gary easily understood that for Barbara, such a connection would serve as an outlet for her strong soprano voice if only her service dog could accompany her into the choir loft. Singing with her healthy vocal cords was its own saving grace for Barbara, as it had been throughout her travels around the world.

Prior to my own retirement as their pastor, I brought Gary and Barbara into a position as Lay Pastor Volunteers for ministry to other sight-impaired members of our local church. They were a couple who handled every challenge as a team. There was no Barbara in ministry without Gary. No Gary in ministry without Barbara. And this symmetry in marriage was especially heightened, I found, following the death of Barbara's service dog, "Kobe." With every application for a new service dog came increased scrutiny of Barbara's own deteriorating health. Could she be ambulatory enough to even move about with the aid of a dog? Her entire body was in a state of decline and increasing weakness. Applications for a new service animal stalled. Barbara's health was failing. And with that her dependency on Gary was seemingly heightened by the day. They would resort to taking in a rescue dog from the pound named Leah, who as an ornery puppy was at best an able distraction; nothing like a service dog, however.

Though no longer their pastor, I would still see Gary and Barbara upon occasion and note that, in Barbara's own weakness, Gary had a unique way of presenting to her his own weaknesses such that Barbara would become again his own strength, his own rescuer. Her health would improve as his went into acute decline, and together they would keep each other strong for as long as at all possible. She would live to help him, and he gave her a means to feel competent and adequate and even healthy amidst her chronic disease. She returned the favor, giving Gary a means to feel competent and adequate as her caretaker. They lived to care for each other.

Because of their unique marriage, Barbara had outlived every medical prediction and prognosis by several years if not decades. Then, at the age of 70, Barbara succumbed to a long and sustained pattern of disease. She died on February 2, 2019.

Every widow is unique in what is to be faced going forward. Every grief is a pain all its own. But when a marriage bond is cemented in a mutual dependency like that of Gary's with Barbara, there is a kind of lonely desperation that may be unrivaled here on earth. Together, Barbara and Gary had each been orphaned, often transplanted between communities, were childless, and so were bound in symmetrical union. Dependent upon each other to the end.

Knowing of Gary's deep state of loneliness, his own faithful and baptized identification with the Christ crucified, and his own moments of Gethsemane isolation, I invited him to describe what it was like for him in those very moments. He wrote these words in reply: ***"The door closed*** *with a gentle thud, the sound of the deadbolt seems a little bit louder, and the bark of my puppy, Leah, seems a bit louder as she welcomes me home as I enter the condo. The only other sound I hear is the television that I had left on to keep her company while I went to church this morning. After muting the television, the only sounds I hear is the ticking of the grandfather's clock and my own heart beating. It has been almost twenty-four hours now since my Barbara left this earth for heaven. It has been quite a bit longer as she spent two months in*

*the Wright Patterson Air Force base hospital since I last heard that beautiful and cheerful greeting when I came through the door. How was I to go on without her? I was scared. What was going to happen tomorrow, and how was I going to manage? I had no-one to lean on as both my and her parents passed away years ago and my sisters live over a day's drive from here and are themselves elderly. I had my Lord and the family at church. That was it. Numbly I made it to the bedroom and laid down as I felt mentally drained. Reality was starting to sink in, and I was balling my heart out. Little Leah snuggled closer and somewhat calmed my heart. I cannot tell you how long I cried, or even why. There are tears of sorrow because you are missing someone, tears also come when one is overjoyed at what has happened to or for a friend or relative. I was crying because Barbara was being missed but also because she was no longer attached to a body that was not as God designed it.*

*Barbara was a very unique person. After leaving her loveless home of abuse and while at a state college she was introduced to Jesus. She would tell people that she never felt so much love bestowed upon her. She also learned to trust people and allow God's Holy Spirit to guide her. She taught me how to have this trust. One of the many things I learned from my wife was that it takes time and a desire to communicate with people to really know them."*

I've asked Gary to help me really know as best I can what his own greatest temptation was while going through his most intense times of loneliness as a new widower. He again chose to place his thoughts in writing: *"**When Barbara passed away, I felt so very alone. My world revolved around me taking care of her and doing those things that she was no longer able to take care of. I was seriously considering cutting all ties with everyone and everything we did together. Without her what was the point. I could blame myself as I was not able to help her keep from getting sick. I could not have kept the abuse she suffered from coming back to weaken her body. I blamed the military for forcing their policies on health care to overrule what we felt was better.**"*

If I can possibly understand or know with any accuracy what Gary may have gone through as a widower, a social role I've never had to personally assume, his greatest temptation at the time of his own Gethsemane of loneliness was to assign blame. Such blame may have started with himself. He may have felt a sense of failure in not being able to prevent her disease and death. He was perhaps tempted to blame a disjointed medical system at points when doctors worked in competition more than collaboration. And the temptation into which he had entered included a kind of, in his words, *"cutting all ties with everyone and everything we did together. Without her what was the point."*

There comes a point where a local church can most easily become disconnected from widows and orphans. It is when the newly single feels surrounded by old couples. This is a point where temptation comes into play. The temptation, as Gary put it, of *"cutting all ties with everyone and everything we did together. Without her what was the point."*

To Gary's own great credit, he did not give into any temptation to wallow in blame or shame involving Barbara's disease and death. He took comfort in the faith that led him into church as a kind of secondary relationship. His primary faith was in God's love.

In his blogpost of August 4, 2010 for **The Gospel Coalition** (https://www.thegospelcoalition.org/), Justin **Taylor** relates a story told by **Dane Ortlund** about a visually impaired Scottish pastor in the late 19th Century named **George Matheson**. Matheson was 20 years old when, as a theological student preparing for the ministry, he was engaged to be married but he was in the process of losing his sight. *"When he broke the news to his fiancé (concerning his prognosis of blindness) she decided she could not go through life with a blind husband. She left him. Before losing his sight, he had written two books of theology and some feel that if he had retained his sight, he could have been the greatest leader of the church of Scotland in his day.*

*A special providence was that George's sister offered to care for him. With her help, George left the world of academia for pastoral ministry and wound-up preaching to 1500 each week despite his blindness.*

*The day came, however, in 1882, when his sister fell in love and prepared for marriage herself. The evening before the wedding, George's whole family had left to get ready for the next day's celebration. He was alone and facing the prospect of living the rest of his life without the one person who had come through for him. On top of this, he was doubtless reflecting on his own aborted wedding day twenty years earlier. It is not hard to imagine the fresh waves of grief washing over him that night.*

*In the darkness of that moment George Matheson wrote this hymn. He remarked afterward that it took him five minutes and that it was the only hymn he ever wrote that required no editing."*

The words of that hymn? Perhaps you will recognize its these first two verses:

*O Love that will not let me go*
*I rest my weary soul in thee*
*I give thee back the life I owe*
*That in thine ocean depths its flow*
*May richer, fuller be.*

*O Light that foll'west all my way*
*I yield my flick'ring torch to thee*
*My heart restores its borrowed ray*
*That in thy sunshine's blaze its day*
*May brighter, fairer be.*

My friend, Gary, found the church ever present during his darkest moments of Gethsemane because his primary faith in God's love would not let him go. Not even where he was most tempted, into an isolated cave of blame and shame over the loss of his dear wife, Barbara. Instead of letting him go, this faith in the light of God's undying love led him into the office of our senior pastor, Rev. Barry Baughman, for some much-needed grief counseling. There Gary was encouraged to do two things as a widower he could never have done while still in the constant care for his dependent wife before her death. The first was to go on a mission trip to our McCurdy Mission in New Mexico, which would surround him in prayer during what amounted to his own lonely garden of Gethsemane. And three months later, he could go on a local 3-day men's retreat sponsored by the United Methodist Church, **"Walk to Emmaus."** (This same retreat exists for women as well, but they are not coed events.)

For those who have never experienced the Emmaus or Cursillo retreat, it recalls for its pilgrim participants the biblical story of two men who were walking from Jerusalem to a village called Emmaus that was some 7 miles away. They were grieving the most recent death of Jesus by crucifixion. Not only so, they were anxiously dealing with the then rumored loss of his buried body that was no longer in its tomb. They were involved in their own *"How was I to go on without [him]? I was scared"* time akin to Gary's own first days without Barbara.

It was, per the biblical Emmaus story, at this point that the resurrected Jesus Christ enters the picture and asks them to explain their lonely grief. Immediately, the men related the known events of recent days involving the death of the one they had previously believed was their rescuer, their Messiah. These men may have thought they already understood what we Christians call the Old Testament Bible. They had their own narrow interpretation of the prophetic writings.

These men on their walk from Jerusalem to Emmaus had their own approach to reading, studying, interpreting their Hebrew Bible. They were missing the general message of God's grace amidst their own habits of narrow understanding. The greater patterns and larger contexts.

When Jesus joined the walk, things changed starting with a new understanding of the scriptures. One that would view the prophetic message not as a list of items for blame and shame, not as a "why couldn't I have prevented this awful crucifixion?" but, instead, as a messianic hope for God's long pattern of extended grace into the final analysis.

The woke church for Gary in his moments of Gethsemane loneliness involved this new way of understanding the scriptures as a whole, not just a series of parts. A broadly connected and rooted forest and not just an assortment of individual trees. A presence of Christ's disciples on a mission team in prayer alongside him. A respite from his greatest temptation to think in his loneliness: *"Without her what was the point. I could blame myself as I was not able to help her keep from getting sick. I could not have kept the abuse she suffered from coming back to weaken her body. I blamed the military for forcing their policies on health care to overrule what we felt was better."*

When Jesus asked his disciples to pray with him that together they not enter into temptation, they instead took naps. The Christ himself was left to deal with his own loneliness. Without his church's supportive presence. As if to identify with the many widows and orphans out there who, despite every indication throughout scripture represent the church's broadest obligation to provide a supportive presence, are left to deal with their own loneliness.

Gary could have been one of them.

He was not because his woke church included not just other members who regularly checked in on him, supplied food for him, and prayed for him. Not just a woke "Pastor Barry" who provided appropriate grief counseling alongside his own prayer for him. But a woke mission team and a woke Emmaus Walk team to pray with him through ongoing days of grief and lonely temptation.

For Gary, and through him for Jesus himself, Gethsemane was redeemed.

Yet, even Gethsemane is never the end of anyone's story. Not the Christ's. Not Gary's. Resurrection comes in perhaps multiple forms, some here on earth. Just ask Jesus.

And just ask Gary.

As if it happened only a week ago, Barbara lives on in Gary's memory of times like when they were stationed with the Air Force in Germany. There God's gift of music was cherished in her ability to sing for their new international friends. In Gary's own words, and with these we can gain closure for this chapter, *"our landlord's father was going to have his 86th birthday party and they wanted to make sure we were going to be there to celebrate. Barb with her little German/English translation guidebook translated the American child's happy birthday song but also sang it to him. There was also the time she sang two numbers in the old Catholic church Latin for the archbishop of Trier when he held the confirmation mass at their base chapel."*

Returning to Ohio's Wright Patterson Air Force Base after Gary's Germany assignment, Barbara joined the Dayton Philharmonic Chorus.

He shares, ***"they performed many pieces of music in their original tongue. That meant she sang in eight different languages."*** And now the memories are shared with those in Gary's own church. Those in his own garden of slowly remitting loneliness.

Gethsemane redeemed.

Chapter 9

I received a letter not long ago from a man I'll simply call Devin.

When he heard what I was writing about, he wanted to make sure I knew of his own story and how it was he had first been abandoned by the church only to be later surrounded in love by what we might agree is now the "woke" church for today's world.

Devin's story goes this way: *"From a young age I knew that I was different from other boys my age in a lot of different ways. As I grew into my teenage body, I began to notice my own feelings about sexuality entering my awareness such that I developed what can only be called a crush on different individuals in my high school. The only problem was that these individuals weren't as different as you might think. Like me they were male. That's right, I was attracted to boys, not girls, like my other male classmates were. I was physically and romantically attracted to only guys."*

At this point in life while looking back on his teen years in the rear-view mirror, Devin notes that he graduated High School in 1989 having never had an actual date with a girl. Strangely, he thought at the time, it wasn't that he was considered unattractive or even unpopular with girls he'd known in class, or even in the church he attended with his family. He knew himself to be well liked, and he considered several girls to be his friends. Some even asked in different ways that he go out on special occasions such as school dances and even the rare drive-in movie during the summer months. *"Always,"* he writes, *"I would come up with what I thought at the time was a clever excuse to say no."* He then adds, *"what I could never tell them or anyone at all was that I found all girls unattractive as far as wanting to be in any sense of the term physically romantic with any of them."* Devin feared not living up to others' expectations or, worst of all, having his secret come out in ways that would reveal what he considered to be crazy crushes he continued having on other boys in his school.

*"My worst loneliness was not, however, on those Friday nights when I would be staying home to avoid being seen as strangely more different than any other guy in our class. Or any other guy my age anywhere."* Devin writes, *"I went to a Pentecostal church with my family and three older siblings. It was there that, while trying to figure out whether my same sex attractions were some temporary aberration or even far worse some deep dark sin that would send me to hell one day, I found myself to be the most unusual kid in church and surely the least likely to be loved and forgiven by the God who as our preacher repeatedly warned us, would judge homosexuality as being an abomination."*

Perhaps you can imagine, as I did upon reading Devin's letter, that he would seek the lowest possible profile within his church congregation so he could avoid notice and escape social as well as spiritual damnation. Perhaps he would find excuses to stay home from church events, worship included, as adroitly as he had escaped having to go out with female peers to which he felt no attraction at all.

That is apparently not what happened.

*"What I learned to do, even before my Senior year of High School, was to volunteer for any work the church needed help with, mostly around the office after I would get out of class during the week. I did everything from sharpen pencils to answer the phone to decorating the platform to get it ready for the next worship service. I found myself interested in working especially wherever adults had gathered to take on an assortment of different tasks in ministry, even with local public housing projects where our church set up food drives and other outreach activities."* Devin continues, *"when it came time to decide a plan for myself after graduation* (from his city's public high school), *I arranged to go in and meet one on one with my church's minister, a man* [I will refer to as Howard even though that wasn't his given name]." It was there that Devin revealed not a peep about anything sexual in his mind or body, but only his felt spiritual call by God to enter the fulltime Christian ministry. *"Howard* (sic) *was most receptive to the news and*

*quick to act in helping me with applications and references both from the high school and the church missionary board so I could attend his alma mater,* (Northwestern) *Bible College."*

*"My next three years of life were spent being fully engaged in my studies in preparation for full-time career in church pastoral ministry. On weekends I would occasionally make the 135-mile drive home to my parents' house where I would again pitch in with any weekend activities at my home church. There was not a day of my life back then when I was not devoted to either my books there on campus or to my services in helping our pastor back home. My roommates in the dorm knew very little about me other than my plans to become a minister and of my spiritual commitment to study to show myself approved as a workman unto the Lord."*

However, all was not well with Devin in those years spent preparing for Christian ministry. He persisted in his two most lonely of pursuits. First, his awareness that the attraction and even lust he felt for certain members of his own sex, one in particular, seemed more and more consuming. All while he interacted with female classmates who occasionally sought him out for a soft drink or even a cafeteria meal after class, never reciprocating with the least bit of romantic interest on his own part. Having to study, work, or otherwise go home for the weekend was his ready excuse to avoid any type of dates with members of the opposite sex.

*I was maybe the worst possible candidate to become a Christian minister. If interviewed for such a position after graduation, they would surely ask about my life as a single man unattached. If a congregation bidding for my services had its own share of single women somewhere in their ranks, I could see the pressure being applied to maybe go out on dates or otherwise have to fend off pursuits by some woman seeing me as an eligible bachelor in her midst. This thought was more than I could possibly bear. My future upon graduation was looking more and more like a nightmare I could not face or cross I could not bear."*

It was at that point, Devin notes in his letter, that he began to view his own future with a kind of heavy pall that made each new day a struggle to address in his own lonely presence. Having prayed to God repeatedly for help in changing his feelings and attractions toward males, asking for healing mercies that would alter his sense of physical desire, Devin contemplated one night in his dorm room an act of suicide that would end his plight and take his secret with him to the grave. If only he had not feared the fires of hell as his then eternal destiny, the temptation might have become his obsession. Finally, feeling in his own mind as if hell was exactly what he deserved and would receive no matter what and when, he made a very unusual effort to seek help from a man reputed by his psychology professor to be a fine counselor.

*"I began to go for weekly counseling sessions, telling this man* [I will call Dr. Smith] *that I was confused about my future because I was depressed and lethargic, which was true in its own peculiar way. But after he pressed me for more information than I had otherwise intended to share, I took a chance and related in one of my meetings with him about finding myself all along being attracted to other males and not to females as God had intended. This is when all hell began to break loose, only it was here on earth. No death by suicide was even required. Because the events of the next three months would drag me into an abyss beyond my worst imaginary dread. Dr. Smith* (sic) *obviously knew my faculty advisor there on campus. Despite what I understood was strict confidentiality, my counselor wrote a letter to my faculty advisor warning him that I must be kept away from any career in church ministry upon graduation."*

As if to further betray what little hope he had left for himself and his future after Bible College, Devin was asked by his home church pastor to meet with him in his study that next Sunday afternoon on a weekend when he was back home and attending a special youth activity he had helped with each year at that time. There Devin walked into an office where the pastor had also, unbeknownst to him, invited his parents to sit in and share in the meeting's agenda. That agenda was simply this: Devin's homosexual desires were now outed within his denomination both in terms of his college faculty and his ordination committee that would be required to consider his application to become a church pastor. He would still be allowed to graduate from the school, but he would be unable to continue his various activities or really any activity in his home church, and the same would apply within their larger denomination. Upon turning to his parents inside the pastor's office in hopes of explaining that he was in every way celibate and was prepared to remain so going forward, they both shifted their attention away from Devin and began asking the pastor's advice on what they should now do. *"Should they still even offer further support as needed financially with my last semester at College? Could they do anything about helping to change his sexual attractions? Was it their fault he had this terrible sin in his life, and if so, which of them was more likely to blame? Was it somehow his father?"* It was at that point that, despairing of his future not just in relation to his career plans and sense of pastoral calling but in relation to his college and then church family, and now even in parents, Devin left that church office and climbed into *"the 1977 Honda Accord I'd purchased through a part-time job in the College chapel as a janitor the past three years."* Tears in his eyes. Heartbreak upon heartbreak, Devin took his own isolated loneliness and its unbearable pain, using it to justify an attempt upon his own life as he drove his car at an apparently high rate of speed into a bridge abutment some twenty or so miles down the nearby interstate highway.

Turning the next page in Devin's rather long and amazing story of near death, I wondered how could this end in any way positive where his faith, and his call to pastoral ministry was concerned. Without his earlier hint of a loving church surrounding his current Reverend title, I'd have thought only to brace myself for another encounter with a lonely Gethsemane figure whose church had let him down.

But he continues, *"I survived my attempt at self-harm and destruction."* And, later in his letter, *"I went on to accept my divorce from the narrow and rigid faith of my youth, taking on a number of secular roles in the hospitality and food service industry. Having been just less than one semester short of graduation from Bible College, I was able to go on and finish a degree from a liberal arts program at a Methodist school not far away."* Only to add further down the page, *"it wasn't easy, and only during my third hotel desk job did I find myself meeting another man who, being gay, was able to meet my long-suppressed desire for a romantic commitment based on both love and physical attraction. Together, and after five years of absence from any form of spiritual faith, we began attending a worship service in a nearby Episcopal Church in the city where we then lived."*

Where his family was concerned, however, his return to this particular part of the Christian faith was scorned. Instead of their support for having finally returned to church, any church, they derided him for his choice of a denomination they considered to be apostate. Never was Devin to bring his partner home to meet any of his relatives. He surmised this was not so much on account of their rejection of his sexual orientation and identity but rather their unending shame if others were to see Devin's sinful state and think ill of their failed parenting in years past. *"They never could decide whether to just blame me or to put it all on themselves."*

In the 9th chapter of John's Gospel, we read about a man who used to sit and beg for handouts near a place called the Pool of Siloam. It was well known by all who passed by that he had been blind since birth. The cause of his blindness was unknown, but that stopped no one, not even the disciples of Jesus, from speculating. They had it narrowed down to two possibilities: either the man or else his parents had sinned. Take your choice.

That these were the only possible causes they could see reflected their own culture as religious Jews in the first century. Jesus, the one his disciples called Rabbi, saw things differently. When asked, his answer was succinct: *"Neither this man nor his parents sinned; he was born blind so that God's works might be revealed in him"* (John 9:3).

Previously (John 8:12) Jesus had proclaimed, *"I am the light of the world. Whoever follows me will never walk-in darkness but will have the light of life."* The Jewish religious leaders, however, were not convinced. Jesus needed an example. And who better to reveal his light than this man, blind from birth, who had known nothing but darkness. And blame. And shame. Reduced to begging for his very survival.

The question was whether, if Jesus were to bring the miracle of light into this blind man's darkness, would the religious folk surrounding him finally change their minds. Would they, in turn, see the light?

This is the context in which Jesus answers, *"Neither this man nor his parents sinned; he was born blind so that God's works might be revealed in him"* (John 9:3). And the context for his miracle of healing. John continues in verse 4, *"We must work the works of him who sent me while it is day; night is coming when no one can work. As long as I am in the world, I am the light of the world." When he had said this, he spat on the ground and made mud with the saliva and spread the mud on the man's eyes, saying to him, "Go, wash in the pool of Siloam." Then he went and washed and came back able to see.*

Here is where the man's neighbors who knew him and his parents would surely take notice and have a change of heart, if not a change of mind.

Right?

I wish.

Turning to verse 8, *The neighbors and those who had seen him before as a beggar began to ask, "Is this not the man who used to sit and beg?" Some were saying, "It is he." Others were saying, "No, but it is someone like him." He kept saying, "I am the man." But they kept asking him, "Then how were your eyes opened?" He answered, "The man called Jesus made mud, spread it on my eyes, and said to me, 'Go to Siloam and wash.' Then I went and washed and received my sight."* Surely this would be the game changer, one might hope. No more would the neighbors look down on either the man or his parents.

But not so fast.

Verse 13: *They brought to the Pharisees the man who had formerly been blind. Now it was a sabbath day when Jesus made the mud and opened his eyes. Then the Pharisees also began to ask him how he had received his sight. He said to them, "He put mud on my eyes. Then I washed, and now I see." Some of the Pharisees said, "This man is not from God, for he does not observe the sabbath." But others said, "How can a man who is a sinner perform such signs?" And they were divided. So, they said again to the blind man, "What do you say about him? It was your eyes he opened." He said, "He is a prophet."*

Finally convinced? Would the religious leaders at least now believe that Jesus was who he claimed to be (*"As long as I am in the world, I am the light of the world."*) because this man blind from birth was no longer in the dark but was able to actually see?

Verse 18: *The Jews did not believe that he had been blind and had received his sight until they called the parents of the man who had received his sight and asked them, "Is this your son, who you say was born blind? How then does he now see?" His parents answered, "We know that this is our son, and that he was born blind; but we do not know how it is that now he sees, nor do we know who opened his eyes. Ask him; he is of age. He will speak for himself." His parents said this because they were afraid of the Jews; for the Jews had already agreed that anyone who confessed Jesus to be the Messiah would be put out of the synagogue. Therefore, his parents said, "He is of age; ask him."*

Notice the bind these parents are now in? They can either stand with their son, as if to say, "if he has to leave the synagogue, so will we." Rather, to preserve their own place in that religious society to which they belonged, they distanced themselves from their own son.

The Pharisees did as his parents asked and allowed. They essentially ganged up on the man and found reason to remove him from the roll of members in good standing within their synagogue. *The man answered, "Here is an astonishing thing! You do not know where he comes from, and yet he opened my eyes. We know that God does not listen to sinners, but he does listen to one who worships him and obeys his will. Never since the world began has it been heard that anyone opened the eyes of a person born blind. If this man were not from God, he could do nothing."⁴ They answered him, "You were born entirely in sins, and are you trying to teach us?" And they drove him out.*

Which brings us back to the story of Devin?

How did things turn out for him, you may wonder? So, when Devin and his partner decided to attend a very different church in their new city of residence, they chose an Episcopal congregation that promised them an open and warm welcome. His letter continues, *"At first, I must be totally honest. It was hard for me to relate my childhood faith to this new faith community. I had trouble trusting that I could ever again belong, feel affirmed, be included as a member of any church family ever again."* Then Devin went on to write about how his own family, as well as his partner's family, continued to keep him....and especially them......at a distance so their own neighbors would not judge them guilty as parents of a gay son. For him, and for his partner, there was no going home again as before. There was only going on again as new. New in Christ. New in the Episcopal Church as members in full, no different than anyone else who would go on to seek God's blessing in the covenant of Holy Matrimony. Which Devin goes on to write about in his letter as the greatest blessing of his lifetime to that point.

Not only that, but there was this to for him to add. *"I found myself engaging the scriptures anew in Bible Study within our new Church and realized I had a Spiritual gift for discerning new meanings afresh within the words of scripture. Also, I was able to then explain them in ways that helped others learn and grow in their own faith."* After some time, Devin felt yet another invitation. It felt warmly familiar to him as being one he'd received during his youthful adolescence. Even as it happened to coincide with his warm feelings of attraction to members, yes, of his same male gender. *"I found myself being called again to follow Christ into the very ministry of shepherding his sheep as a minister of the Gospel. God was calling me to be his witness from the pulpit, to be his representative in bringing good news of God's healing love for all who need the heavenly grace and truth that passes, far too often, our human understanding."*

*"Today,"* Devin writes in conclusion, *"it is me that is serving as a seminary graduate and ordained diocesan Priest within the local parish to which my husband and I have been appointed. I feel surrounded in love by my affirming and encouraging and faithful community. And accompanied in common prayer by a church that I always needed but never had. A church that is there for me where before my painful loneliness ruled over my very faith. And, by irony, it is the pastor of my youth who has left the ordained ministry and is working in secular roles to make his own living back in my home community. He, too, has been driven out of that church and denomination."*

Therein lives the Gethsemane redeeming story of Pastor Devin. Reverend Devin, as his picture near the parish marque notes in enclosure with his letter to me. It is a story of sensed abandonment followed by one of restored fellowship. A story of darkness from birth that could now see the light. A story of one driven out only to now be drawn in as never before.

Which takes us back to that Bible story. The one involving the man blind from birth but now able to see by the light of Jesus. As we read in verse 35: ***Jesus heard that they had driven him out, and when he found him, he said, "Do you believe in the Son of Man?" He answered, "And who is he, sir? Tell me, so that I may believe in him." Jesus said to him, "You*** *have seen him, and the one speaking with you is he." He said, "Lord, I believe." And he worshiped him. Jesus said, "I came into this world for judgment so that those who do not see may see, and those who do see may become blind"* (John 9:35-39).

*Chapter 10*

Daniel Patrick Sheehan, in his November 16, 2019 report for The Morning Call section of Pennsylvania's **"Lehigh Valley News,"** shares a story about a "woke" church in that area. It involved a child with autism, whose mother brought him with her to visit the worship space of St. John's United Church of Christ in the town of Emmaus.

If you've raised a child with some level of autism disease, you may appreciate the courage with which this particular mother ventured into a setting as formal as a Christian sanctuary worship service. In a pew occupied by only one individual, the mother and son approached somewhat apologetically to ask that person's permission to sit there. That person just happened to be Kevin Snyder, a member of St. John's who had a wife, Beryl, singing in the choir that day.

Per Sheehan's report, the mother whispered *"that her son had autism and warned that he might be disruptive during the service. No worries, he assured her. Soon, the boy began fidgeting. The mother apologized. Honestly, Snyder told her, it's no bother. The boy kept fidgeting. And the mother, clearly embarrassed, took him and left."*

Aw, the loneliness of this mother's Gethsemane.

Like Jesus in his own garden, she asked. But then she left and went away. Perhaps to pray on her own.

Such scenes happen in churches all over the world, I suppose. Parents try. Maybe even more than once or twice, only to give up and go their own separate way. Whatever temptations are theirs to enter, they do their praying alone. And whatever sweating of blood, as the metaphor goes, is done in private. Disconnected from whatever church remains at peaceful rest.

The initial disconnect between Jesus and his church at Gethsemane is still going on in our world today.

But it doesn't have to be that way.

And it didn't remain that way at St. John's United Church of Christ in Emmaus, Pennsylvania back in 2019.

Sheehan continues in this report, when *"Beryl Snyder heard the story, it troubled her. She was even more disturbed later when one of the staff members at the church…shared an article that said an extraordinarily high percentage of parents with autistic children seldom or never attend services because their children might cause disruptions. She didn't know much about autism. She set to work anyway, looking for ideas to make the church more welcoming to parents who were depriving themselves of the kind of spiritual sustenance that might ease the stress of raising children with autism. Fidgeting and tantrums among children in church are hardly confined to autistic children, of course. They are more common because autism is a sensory disorder, meaning lights, textures and sounds can prove especially distressing."*

Autism, as you might know, is one of the fastest growing developmental disorders in America.

What to do?

Beryl Snyder at first didn't know, but that didn't stop her from working hard enough to find out. And what she found in way of answers and solutions came not at first from other churches but, of all places, a museum in the town of Reading, Pennsylvania that developed a Certified Autism Center for children eager to learn and grow in their own unique methods. Among their offerings to such youngsters upon museum entry were "tactile sensory bags," which contain items designed to soothe and engage autistic children, including headphones to block out noise and sunglasses to dim lights.

As Sheehan then reports, Beryl Snyder wondered why the St. John's Church could not do something like that as well. Why couldn't autistic children find something in a "tactile sensory bag" to keep them occupied during an adult worship service? And as the report continues, Beryl *"followed the museum's lead, including headphones and sunglasses in the bags. Other items include soft gloves, Beanie Babies — 'These are fun to just squish,' she said — and light-up fidget spinners. Oh, and Twiddle Muffs."* And more.

Then came the use of a glass paneled and more sound-proof "Quiet Room" for parents of fussy children and crying infants where the service could be heard by adults while children played with plush toys and colorful books, as needed.

Resources being made ready; it was time for the test.

From the Good Shepherd Rehabilitation Hospital in their area came a young couple, Kevin and Ashley, whose 4-year-old autistic child was able to communicate mostly by pointing and saying the first letter of each word in a sentence. An example of his functional abilities involves his ability to correlate letters and numbers. Dad says E, for instance, and the child easily and immediately points to the number 5 on the wall calendar. He says X, his son points to 24 on the calendar, and so on.

Early in November of 2019 Kevin and Ashley were ready. They came to church. Along with their, at times loudly exuberant child who was almost always in motion. As Sheehan reported,

*"thanks to Beryl Snyder's bags of goodies and the welcoming quiet room, she found the spiritual haven she had denied herself for a long time. The young boy occupied himself. His mother sang and prayed.*

*And Snyder saw a church where many more [families] could make a home on Sunday, not only for their benefit but for the enlightenment of the congregation itself. Autism, after all, remains a mystery to many people."*

Isn't this an example of what a woke church would do in our age of loneliness?

Isn't this what the sheep, noting once again that Jesus-parable of Matthew 25, were credited with doing? *"Truly I tell you, just as you did it to one of the least of these who are members of my family, you did it to me."*

Isn't this an example of what redeeming Gethsemane looks like in today's world?

In the 5th chapter of Mark, we read about another parent of another child. And of another request made by the parent before almost giving up and going away like the mother who inspired the transformation of St. John's UCC in Emmaus, PA. In that Markan account of Jesus's life, the parent was named Jairus.

It seemed Jairus knew Jesus and asked his help, possibly, in the saving of his young daughter's life. As Jesus was going with Jairus to hopefully heal the very sick child, he found himself interrupted by other persons begging also for some acts of healing. If you've ever had to wait in line at a doctor's office past your own appointment time, you know the drill. Healing is not always without interruptions; some longer than others.

This time, according to the biblical account, Jesus's interruption was much longer than anticipated. Jairus was still waiting for Jesus when he got the message. Someone from his house where the little girls was lingering came with the report (Mark 5:35), *"Your daughter is dead. Why trouble the* healer (Jesus) *any further?"*

Flashback to that scene inside the St. John's sanctuary the Sunday when a mother with child, afflicted by autism, left the pew where Kevin Snyder sat wanting to help.

No doubt many a Dad or Mom has left a church service before, escorting their sick child, feeling like a bother, and giving up hope. And go home to weep. And to pray in the loneliness and emptiness of their own Gethsemane about the cup from which they must drink.

As Mark's story of Jairus unfolds, Jesus reacted along the same lines as Beryl Snyder of St. John's UCC in Emmaus, PA nearly two thousand years later. *"But overhearing what they said, Jesus said to (Jairus) 'Do not fear, only believe.' He allowed no one to follow him except Peter, James, and John, the brother of James. When they came to the house of (Jairus), he saw a commotion, people weeping and wailing loudly. When he had entered, he said to them, 'Why do you make a commotion and weep? The child is not dead but sleeping.' And they laughed at him. Then he put them all outside and took the child's father and mother and those who were with him and went in where the child was. He took her by the hand and said to her.... 'little girl, get up!' And immediately the girl got up and began to walk about......"* (Mark 5:36-43).

I find it interesting that Jesus took Peter, James, and John with him to heal the child in this story. And to redeem the grieving father amidst his own moments of anxiety, blood, sweat, and tears.

These were the same church (charter) members Jesus took with him to that garden of Gethsemane later on in his own age of loneliness. The ones who, at his side, were found not to be dead but only sleeping.

Is the church today dead?

No.

But like Peter, James and John, and the young daughter of Jairus, the church is too often sleeping.

Were Jesus to take the church today by the hand, I wonder if he wouldn't say something to the same effect of ***"little girl, get up!"*** I wonder if Jesus is still not calling for his disciples to wake up. Hoping that we, like the daughter of Jairus, might immediately get up and walk about.

The time to redeem Gethsemane is now. The age of loneliness is at hand. And as often as we join the least of these who are children of God, we are joining with the Christ himself who asked his church to pray about the drinking of that cup and the temptation not to. It wasn't just his cup. Not just the cup which parents like Kevin and Ashley must drink.

It is our cup, too. ***"Drink, ye, all of it."***

And now back once again to that St. John's United Church of Christ in the biblically named Lehigh Valley town of Emmaus. Daniel Patrick Sheehan concluded his report for his newspaper's section, The Morning Call, with this message of genuine wokeness. *"I love when people ask me questions,' said Ashley, who became a devoted evangelist of the autism awareness movement."* Beryl Snyder, too, *"is trying to get the word out through social media and word of mouth: All children welcome. 'If this would take off, and I really hope it does, I would love to get more children and parents back to church,' she said. 'I want them to find a spiritual home.'"*

# CONCLUSION

Do you remember the story of Sarah as shared in Chapter Six?

It was the night before she was to encounter a high-risk cranial surgery to remove possibly malignant polyps discovered near her brain. She was a lonely seminary student. She'd requested prayer from the choir at church, but then heard nothing from anyone until that night before. She was, let's say, then tempted to not drink that cup. Thought of cancelling her next day's surgery.

Which is when Alycia, one of the other choir members, came by to visit and pray with her.

Sarah was comforted in two ways that night by Alycia. First, of course, was her being there in her own age of loneliness to pray lest she cave to the temptation of calling the whole thing off instead of going through the dreaded surgery that next day. She felt a sense of community with her church like never before.

Secondly, Sarah felt lovable again much in the same way as Martha's sister, Mary, was loved by Jesus in that story of Luke 10:38-42, the very story that follows Jesus's parable of the Good Samaritan. Sarah had what felt to her like a Jesus' visit with someone who didn't mind sitting on a sofa with cat hairs or moving aside all the books and papers scattered about.

I left that story of Sarah's unfinished.

Just as the Good Samaritan might have continued his friendship with the fallen victim beyond the time of his recovery at the inn (paid for by the Samaritan), and just as Martha's sister, Mary, continued to care for Jesus past the point of Jesus's visit also in Luke 10, so Alycia continued to care for Sarah. And Sarah for Alycia.

You see, after graduating from seminary with her D.Min., Sarah married Kevin LaRose, the love of her life. For the wedding she needed bridesmaids. And Sarah's first choice was Alycia, who served with her customary grace.

Yet, that's not the end either.

Several years went by. Years of close friendship.

Alycia's own daughter was getting married. For that wedding she needed a pastor. And the daughter's first choice was Pastor Sarah, Mom's close friend dating back to that dark and lonely night before surgery. When Sarah's own Gethsemane was redeemed.

This story of Sarah and Alycia and their woke "Mary" church is still going on today and will make its way into Sarah's own eventual book of memoirs. By the way, Sarah has been visually impaired and legally blind from early childhood. She has been reading Braille since the age of 5. Always blind and often alone, but never disabled and no longer lonely. She's learned a great deal about life and now is a college professor with a great deal to teach others. I can hardly wait to read her own memoirs!

Years ago, when I was a college kid trying to learn more about life myself, perhaps my strangest lesson was that I was no good at hitchhiking. Not even close. Never saw even one "brake light" go by.

It was among those things of which I can say, "tried it once, and that was enough." I learned upon that one occasion that I could walk a lot farther than I thought I could.

But that wasn't all.

That day as I stood in the cold, brisk Kansas wind poking my thumb out in the direction of all oncoming cars facing me, I learned that hitchhiking can be a long pursuit into loneliness. I only needed to go to the nearest town 10 miles away. I knew that on this particular highway, most of those passing by me were headed for that very same town, the Rice County-seat. I knew I was harmless. I was skinny and had ridden in the back seat of a VW bug before. I wouldn't need much room. Even the back of a pickup truck would've been fine. Just a ride into the next town.

Please?

But no one stopped. And although I was off on the side shoulder of the road with my thumb in the air, some even crossed over to the other side of the two-lane highway to pass by me as if I was some kind of a Kansas farm implement hogging their space. Or maybe they thought I was some jailbird on the loose? No one seemed to understand that I was not there to hurt anyone. I just wanted someone to stop and give me a ride.

No one stopped. Or even slowed down. Not even one brake light or sign of consideration.

And in those moments, I got a glimpse, pre-seminary student that I was, of what it may have felt like in some very tiny way to be the victim in Christ's parable of the Good Samaritan. As everyone passed me by, I felt a kind of almost bitter loneliness inside. I felt misunderstood. And, actually, now that I reflect back on the experience, kind of unlovable.

Jesus had many parables that in some way or another touched on love, and also on the experience of loneliness. The kind of loneliness that could cause one to feel unlovable. Yet, no parable from any of the synoptic Gospels quite measures up to that of the Good Samaritan when it comes to the experience of loneliness.

You remember that story, don't you?

*"A man was going down from Jerusalem to Jericho, and fell into the hands of robbers, who stripped him, beat him, and went away, leaving him half dead. Now by chance a priest was going down that road; and when he saw him, he passed by on the other side. So likewise, a Levite, when he came to the place and saw him, passed by on the other side. But a Samaritan while traveling came near him; and when he saw him, he was moved with pity. He went to him and bandaged his wounds, having poured oil and wine on them. Then he put him on his own animal, brought him to an inn, and took care of him. The next day he took out two denarii, gave them to the innkeeper, and said, "Take care of him; and when I come back, I will repay you whatever more you spend"* (Luke 10:30-35).

If viewed as allegories, there is a role for each one of us to play in several of the Christ parables. Been passed by before? Been a lonely and neglected victim before? The good Samaritan knew how that felt. No wonder he made the perfect person to stop and care for the victim in that story. Hurt people often are the first to help people.

Unfortunately, too many of us even in today's church would, if altogether honest, fit the role of the religious leaders who passed by on the other side of that fallen victim along the Jericho road. We've played that part even as we've played the part of those three disciples who slept amidst the worst time of loneliness Jesus ever suffered. We've all been negligent before.

Most of the Christ parables identified a sinner somewhere in the story. The lost sheep? That's been me before, lost by means of my own refusal to follow the good shepherd in the first place. Prodigal son? That's been me before, having to swallow pride and return home on my own because, left to only my own devices, I wasn't enough. The older brother? That's been me, reluctant to forgive someone else who had obviously messed up bigtime.

I've seen both sides of loneliness myself. I've been with and without the church upon entering into my own Gethsemane temptations. And, yes,

I've been asleep at the switch before when I should've been awake and praying with those like Sarah in that previous story.

Loneliness is far worse than just a few individual stories here and there. Worse than a hitchhiker who never catches a ride to wherever. It has, by some estimates, become something of a global pandemic in its own right. Whatever can be written about the pandemic of Covid-19 might also need to be written about loneliness, one of Covid's most glaring of complications. To some degree, ours has now become most everyone's age of loneliness.

One of the most powerful pieces ever written about loneliness came from Nicholas Kristof, one of my favorite syndicated columnists. Writing for the **New York Times** on November 9, 2019, well before the current Covid-19 arrived, he addressed the issue. He noted in his column that social *"isolation is more lethal than smoking 15 cigarettes a day, or than obesity, according to research published by Julianne Holt-Lunstad of Brigham Young University. Since obesity is associated in the United States with 300,000 to 600,000 deaths a year, the implication is that loneliness is a huge, if silent, killer. Professor Holt-Lunstad has found that greater social connection is associated with a 50 percent reduced risk of early death.*

Kristof continues.

*Loneliness increases inflammation, heart disease, dementia and death rates, researchers say — but it also simply makes us heartsick and leaves us inhabiting an Edvard Munch canvas. Public health experts in many countries are debating how to address a 'loneliness epidemic' that corrodes modern life, but Britain has taken the lead…. by appointing a minister for loneliness in 2018."*

Kristof adds this quote from Dr. Vivek Murthy, who was surgeon general of the United States under President Barack Obama, *"I trained in internal medicine, and I expected most of my time would be spent on diabetes or heart disease or cancer. What I didn't expect was that so many people I saw would be struggling with loneliness."*

To end that day's column, Kristof poses a most interesting question: *"Maybe the United States, too, should experiment: How about a new post in the Department of Health and Human Services — an assistant secretary for loneliness?"*

To end my own writing on this same issue, I'd like to pose a similar question.

How about if we who still serve within the Church of Jesus Christ of Nazareth appoint ourselves as "ministers for loneliness?"

How about if we do it for the least of these who are members of God's family? How about thereby doing it for Jesus? How about redeeming Gethsemane?

Surely, we can enter someone else's age of loneliness, someone else's time of temptation, someone else's garden of Gethsemane. Surely, we can be a woke church in this time of global loneliness, the all too silent pandemic now among us.

Jesus left most of his parables open-ended in some fashion. It was his way of starting the Kingdom we would be counted on to finish.

Counted on to be his church.

His church in a very different way.

The church as in the older brother who, after hearing his Dad's plea, mulls the matter over a while and then changes his mind. Then going in and joining the banquet, putting his arms around that younger prodigal brother and saying, *"welcome home, bro! Great to have you back. We've all messed up before in one way or another. You don't need to feel lonely any longer."*

The church that says to Jesus, the Good Shepherd, *"don't worry. You stay here with the 90 and 9. We'll go out and find the lost sheep and bring him back to the fold."* And upon finding that lost sheep? Surely, we can be the woke church saying to that lonely one, *"don't worry. We're here now. We're going to stay with you until we all get back to the Good Shepherd where we all belong. And where we'll all be together again as God's family."*

No more loneliness for the least of these? No more loneliness for Jesus?

That's the challenge for today's church. It's our next wake-up call from the Master.

# DISCUSSION QUESTIONS

Week One ……. read Chapters One and Six

- Read Mark 1:40-45

- How did having a communicable disease contribute to loneliness during the time Jesus was conducting his ministry? How might it have been even worse than having a mental illness at that time? Do you think the same might be true in our time as well? Explain.

- What do you think drew Jesus to focus on helping lonely and isolated people as he began his ministry, according to Mark's first chapter?

- Have you ever experienced loneliness at a level where you felt misunderstood, ignored or even avoided by people in church? How easily do we in the church today forget what it was like for ourselves when lonely?

- When Erik, the former hospital chaplain, faced loneliness without the support of church friends, he turned to hiking and photography amidst the out of doors. And then he started a Facebook group for the fellowship he may have missed from no longer attending church services. He is no longer seeking any connection with the church, though he does profess an ongoing faith in Jesus. How may the church have possibly gone wrong in relation to Erik?

- Do you agree that churches may too often act more like Martha in the story of Luke 10:38-42? If so, why might that be?

- Both Erik and Sarah had church backgrounds and even seminary education in common, but there are several differences to note as well. Perhaps the most important was the action taken by Alycia to share in Sarah's worst time of loneliness. If you were in Erik's church and knew of his divorce, his homelessness and then unemployment, how might you have been able to make a difference in his life?

- How can a Mary church go about doing the right things in our age of loneliness?

Prayer: Loving God, we thank you for your call in our lives to do the right things. Forgive us for those times when we become too caught up in doing everything just right for you. Grant our hearts the courage to trust in your grace. Help us extend your same grace to others, knowing this is the right thing to do in our world of human imperfection. And in doing the right thing, may we each one touch the very heart of some lonely person this week. Amen.

Week Two ……. read Chapters Two and Seven

- Read Matthew 12:12-13. If Jesus were to enter our church buildings today, would he take objection to what he finds?

- Have you, like Linda, ever felt a sense of loneliness while seeking to solve problems of social injustice in the world? Why might people like Jesus, turning the tables in an unjust world instead of just talking about it, become unjust victims of loneliness themselves?

- Pastor Linda found herself well engaged in the social action and benevolence ministries of her local church, but assuming the pastoral role of her own small church brought her into positions of conflict and consequential loneliness. Do pastors facing conflict risk a similar disillusionment and painful sense of burnout? How can a church address such a risk in support of pastors who face lonely temptations to leave the ministry?

- What might a church do to maintain connection with all persons of passion and high levels of idealism? Should the church reach out in any way to those past servants now suffering a lonely sense of burnout?

- Where Linda presents a story of one whose loneliness was driven by her church experience, Pat presents an opposite story of one whose loneliness was driven away by her church. Where Linda's passion for social justice was discouraged by her church, Pat's passion for transporting children to church and fixing broken equipment was encouraged by hers. How might today's church best understand and then connect with the individual passions of each member in order to create more connections and fewer disconnects like Linda experienced?

- Read Judges 4:4-10. How could you describe Deborah's passion for justice? How is it that God was able to affirm her passion and use it to save the people of Israel from their 20-year oppression at the hands of King Jabin of Canaan?

- Do "strong women" ever meet with resistance among those who speak for today's church? If so, what causes that to happen? If not, what keeps that from happening? How can the church be helpful in supporting those like Judge Deborah in today's world?

Prayer: Prophetic God, we thank you for your call in our lives to do justice. Forgive us for those times when we talk about injustice but do little about it. Grant our hearts the courage to affirm those who would lead us beyond our own traditions and comforts. Help us to extend your prophetic voice and disruptive action into our world of human indifference. And in doing justice, may we each one touch the very heart of some lonely person this week. Amen.

Week Three ……. Chapters 3 and 8

- Read Matthew 15:1-15. What example did Jesus set for his disciples, and the religious leaders of their day, of how to go about reading their Bible? How had those same leaders used the sanitary laws of Moses to exclude people in that time and place? How might that have affected women and children, those in need of healthcare, those in need of food?

- How did Jesus use a book of Prophecy to interpret a book of Law according to Matthew 15? In reading our Bible, can we as disciples today learn from Jesus a better way of interpreting the Law and Prophets of our Old Testament? How might that affect how we deal with persons like Betty and her child in facing our own legal system?

- Read Matthew 15:21-28. Why didn't Jesus ignore the Syrophoenician mother in this story as his own religious tradition and scriptures might have advised? Would we ever ignore such a foreign mother and child upon begging at our national border? In what way was Betty's approach to her Christian faith similar to that of the Syrophoenician mother in this story? Are we ever inclined by scripture or tradition to ignore those like Betty in our current world?

- In what way might Betty's own church have better attended to her own "age of loneliness" inside their own community courtroom?

- In the story of Gary and his wife, we read that Barbara's service dog for the blind was not allowed in some church sanctuaries. Does this raise any issues for today's church leaders in the care of persons having service dogs? What can we learn from these service dogs that might help us in ministry to the lonely of our communities?

- Read Acts 6:1-6.  This passage informs the diaconal ministry of Christian churches throughout history.  Notice the importance of ministry to the widowed community in particular.  How might Paul and other Apostles have applied the interpretation of scripture best exemplified by Jesus himself?

-  Do we as today's church sometimes do a better job of caring for the single widowed individual than the single divorced individual?  How is the age of loneliness the same or different for each of these individuals?  How can the church better attend to the needs of both individuals?  How can a woke church help both the Betty's and Gary's in our midst?

Prayer:  Discerning God, we thank you for your call in our lives to bear one another's burdens.  Forgive us for those times when we privilege the haves and marginalize the have nots among us.  Grant our hearts the courage to support all who have suffered loss.  Help us to extend your comforting presence wherever there is felt absence in our world of human grief.  And in sharing burdens, may we each one touch the very heart of some lonely person this week.  Amen.

Week Four .........Chapters 4 and 9

- The very different stories of Jake and then Devin bring up questions about the adolescent quest for a meaningful adult vocation. Both have faced different obstacles in their path. Both faced much loneliness as a result of these obstacles. Both faced a temptation to even end their lives due to such loneliness and despair. Do you find such stories to be highly unusual? Why? Why not?

- Read Galatians 6:9-10. Have you known anyone who struggled at wanting to *"help people better themselves"* or *"do good to all people"* only to then feel hopeless and meaningless in their earthly labors? Is there a role for the church to play in connecting with such an individual? Explain.

- Have you known other individuals who struggled to avoid the fatigue of helping other people? Are there people today who *"become weary in doing good?"* Is there a role for the church to play in connecting with such an individual? Explain.

- Where did Jake's home church sleep through their own opportunity to connect with Jake after he left college? Is it always best for local churches to wait for young adults to reach out to them, especially if they are feeling despair while in a foreign country, as Jake was experiencing? Can you imagine a scenario in which Jake's age of loneliness could have met up with a woke church?

- Read John 9:1-5. The author ties this story of the man born blind with the story of Devin born gay. Is there a valid comparison between the visually impaired community in Jesus's day and the LGBTQ community in our own? How did the religious folks of

John 9 and the religious folks of Devin's home church tend to view blindness and homosexuality, respectively?

- Where did Devin's home church sleep through their own opportunity to connect with Devin and his parents while he was still in college? How common is it, do you suppose, for the parents of LGBTQ children to feel blame or shame in relation to their local church? How would you like to see the church handle such issues in today's world?

- Without a doubt, homosexuality was present during the time of the Christ's own ministry of healing. Of all the conditions presented to him with a request for healing, why would you imagine no one of his own LGBTQ community ever was brought to him for healing? Is it possible Jesus regarded sexuality as something that needed no repair or change apart from not lusting after another person outside of marriage? Why? Why not?

Prayer: Inclusive God, we thank you for your call in our lives to affirm others' noble intentions. Forgive us for those times when we judge others because of whom they might love. Grant our hearts the courage to embrace all who would help others better themselves. Help us to extend your own covenant with all who would offer love, wherever and to whomever that might be in our world of human insecurity. And in affirming all helpers and lovers, may we each one touch the very heart of some lonely person this week. Amen.

Week Five .........Chapters 5 and 10

- Read Acts 10:34-48. This is the story of the Gentile Pentecost. In what way is it the same as the story of the Jewish Pentecost in Acts 2? In what way is it different?

- What is the risk we take when expecting others to come to us and join with us instead of traveling to them, like Peter and the early church did upon traveling to Caesarea to join with the Gentiles? Would we be Christians today if the early church had waited for the Gentiles to come to Jerusalem and assimilate with the church there?

- What are some things God has made clean that we may still label as "profane" and seek to avoid today? Where the issue of protest marches for social justice are concerned, what is the risk the church takes if we avoid going to be with those like Jo when inviting our support?

- Is it possible that communities, like families, can become dysfunctional in ways that prevent necessary problem solving and community protection? The author implies that the church must join with the community, like a therapist must join the family, before it can effectively help the community re-organize to solve its problems. If that might be the case, then what are some other ways the church can join a problem-community and first "assimilate" with them?

- In the story of St. John's Church, the first step began with a failure. The mother of an autistic church left the worship service and never returned. How common might this failure be on the part of other churches today?

- Read Mark 5:35-42. The comparison is made between Jairus's daughter and today's church that neither are dead, but rather just asleep. How can Jesus take the hand of today's church and help us get up and walk again?

- What did St. John's Church do that our church could also do in awakening to the needs of lonely and isolated families in our own community? How can our church get up like Jairus's daughter and do unto the least of these in ways that will help redeem Gethsemane?

Prayer: Missionary God, we thank you for your call in our lives to assimilate with others. Forgive us for those times when we wait for others to come and join with us as Christians. Grant our hearts the courage to wake up, go out, join with those who are different from us. Help us to extend your mission and put aside any labels and fears in our world of human diversity. And in joining with others where they are, may we each one touch the very heart of some lonely person this week. Amen.

Week Six ………. Introduction and Conclusion

DISCUSSION

- Read Mark 14:32-42. Jesus demonstrates that private prayer and corporate prayer are both important for us as Christians. Have you experienced this same importance in your own life? Describe the different needs you have felt for prayer. When have you most welcomed someone in the church being present with you in prayer?

- Jesus asked for the church to be with him while in prayer. Have you ever hesitated to ask for the church to pray with you?

- What temptations were most real in the lives of both Jesus and his church as they faced coming events? Are there still temptations facing the church today that require our corporate prayer as communities of faith?

- Have you ever experienced a time of loneliness even in the presence of your own church? Is it possible you have under-estimated someone else's loneliness even when gathered together as a church? How might we at times identify with Jesus at Gethsemane? How might we at times identify with the disciples?

- Read Luke 10:30-35. Have you ever experienced life in some degree like that of the victim in the Good Samaritan story? Have you ever experienced life like the religious leaders in that same story? Have you ever experienced life like the Good Samaritan who stopped for some other lonely soul along your journey?

- Do you agree or disagree that loneliness is an "all too silent pandemic among us" today? How can the church be more intentional in its outreach to those so afflicted as to damage their own health-outcomes? Would becoming "ministers for loneliness" serve a healing and redemptive purpose in today's world?

- Were the church today in the role of older brother to the prodigal son, how might we change our ways to become atoned with those we have previously resented? Is God still calling us to wake up, watch out, and pray with? It is too late for the church to redeem Gethsemane and awaken to new resurrection, no matter our past?

Prayer: Reconciling God, we thank you for your call in our lives to wake up, watch out and pray with others. Forgive us for those times when we have missed or dismissed someone else's age of loneliness. Grant our hearts the courage to rise up and attend to the temptations of those now in despair. Help us to extend your redemption of those who have felt abandoned in our world of human brokenness. And in redeeming the least of these who are now broken, may we each one redeem Gethsemane as your church in service for Jesus Christ, who is crucified and risen in service for all the world. Amen.

**Other titles from Higher Ground Books & Media:**

Love's Resurrection: Its Power to Roll Away Fear's Heaviest Stone

by Daniel K. Held

The Power of Knowing by Jean Walters

Wise Up to Rise Up by Rebecca Benston

Forgiven and Not Forgotten by Terra Kern

Through the Sliver of a Frosted Window by Robin Melet

Knowing Affliction and Doing Recovery by John Baldasare

Out of Darkness by Stephen Bowman

Breaking the Cycle by Willie Deeanjlo White

Healing in God's Power by Yvonne Green

Chronicles of a Spiritual Journey by Stephen Shepherd

The Real Prison Diaries by Judy Frisby

My Name is Sam…And Heaven is Still Shining Through by Joe Siccardi

The Words of My Father by Mark Nemetz

The Bottom of This by Tramaine Hannah

Add these titles to your collection today!

http://www.highergroundbooksandmedia.com

**Do you have a story to tell?**

Higher Ground Books & Media is an independent Christian-based publisher specializing in stories of triumph! Our purpose is to empower, inspire, and educate through the sharing of personal experiences.

Please visit our website for our submission guidelines.

http://www.highergroundbooksandmedia.com

www.ingramcontent.com/pod-product-compliance
Lightning Source LLC
Chambersburg PA
CBHW071702040426
42446CB00011B/1877